THE SYSTEMS THINKING APPROACH™

TO

CREATING THE PEOPLE EDGE

THROUGH

STRATEGIC HUMAN

RESOURCE MANAGEMENT

Strategic People Planning:

An
Executive Briefing
on
People Edge Best Practices

Your Personal Briefing Booklet and Workbook

Fourth Edition

1420 Monitor Road • San Diego • California • 92110-1545 • (619) 275-6528 • Fax (619) 275-0324

Copyright © 2005
2nd Edition - 4th Revision
Systems Thinking Press®
Library of Congress Control Number: 2005932190
ISBN: 0-9760135-5-X

> People are the engine
> Not the fuel to be used up.

The Centre "Nothing to Lose" Guarantee
How to Get Started on Your Strategic People Planning or People-Edge Change Project
"Value-Added" One Day Meeting

Dear Participant:

As a way to get started on your Customer-Focused Strategic People Planning and "People Edge" Change Project, we usually recommend a one-day Executive briefing and Plan-to-Plan session with the Centre for Strategic Management®. In this one day, we are both able to educate each other on (1) strategic people planning, (2) creating the People Edge, or (3) any large scale change project you are planning to implement. It also allows us to get on the "same sheet of music" as to your situation. We will also mutually analyze, decide, and tailor what type of strategic planning or change management project, if any, should go beyond this one day event.

We are so confident of our ability to help you in this one day that we offer a "Nothing to Lose" Guarantee for this event with your top management team. If you do not get a "Value-Added" day from the time we spend together, pay us our expenses only and the day's fee is waived.

In addition, there is no obligation beyond the one day . . . both parties have to agree that there is mutual benefit to proceed further.

This booklet includes the handouts and overheads we use in this 1-day session. As a prework to this Booklet and Plan-to-Plan Day, we highly recommend you first read our 4-page Executive Summary Article on this topic. Without the article, this booklet will not be as useful and user friendly to you. If you need a copy of this article, please call us at the Centre.

Happy Reading,

Stephen S. Haines

Stephen G. Haines
President
San Diego, California
(619) 275-6528

hrmcover.pmd

1420 Monitor Road • San Diego • California • 92110-1545 • (619) 275-6528 • Fax (619) 275-0324

WHY IS THE "PEOPLE EDGE" IMPORTANT TO YOU?

1. **"Blinding Flash of the Obvious" (BFO):**
   - Everything in an organization is inert, it takes people to run them and make things happen.
   - The People Edge is difficult to create and sustain; making it the one competitive edge that can really differentiate you in today's "commodity" world.

2. AQF and Ernst & Young did a **massive study on profitability:**
   - Four countries
   - Four big industries
   - Only three things always increased profitability:
     - #1: Developing and deploying **a Strategic Plan**
     - #2: Increasing your **range and depth of leadership and management practices**
     - #3: **Improving your business processes including people proceses** (lowering costs as long as they are still customer-driven)

3. **HR Study/Best Practices:**

> **Human Resource Practices
> Do Make a Difference in Corporate Performance**
>
> Companies using the best HR practices
> show both a higher degree of productivity
> and stronger market performance
>
> Source: Society for Human Resource Management and CCH Limited Survey

The research is in:
Employers that score in the top 25% for quality HR practices also have superior index ratings for productivity, market value and sales performance.

It is just plain good business practice to do this!

hrmcover.pmd

1420 Monitor Road • San Diego • California • 92110-1545 • (619) 275-6528 • Fax (619) 275-0324

CREATING THE PEOPLE EDGE
① to **①A** to **②** to **③**

❶ Strategic Edge

①A

Exec/Employee Development Board

Facilitation of Strategic Management:
- Strategic Planning
- Change Management

"Strategic Business Design"

❷ People Edge	❸ Customer Edge
Attunement With People:	**Alignment of Delivery:**
• Strategic People Plan/ Mgmt.	• Positioning for Value
• Ldrshp Development System ❷ Supports ❸ ➔	• Organization Redesign
• Succession/Careers	• Process Improvement
• Hiring/Workforce Planning	• Technology/Tools
• Performance Management	• Quality Products & Services
• Rewards/Recognition	• Operational Tasks
• Coach/Empl. Involvement	• Team Work
• Cultural Change	• Blow-Out Bureaucracy

Greater Choice

Faster Response

Better Service

Customer Value

Lower Cost

Higher Quality

--- **Our Foundation** ---

❹ The Systems Thinking Approach™
and
Strategic Communications — Shared Vision, Values and Strategies

hrmcover.pmd

1420 Monitor Road • San Diego • California • 92110-1545 • (619) 275-6528 • Fax (619) 275-0324

THE ABCs OF
STRATEGIC PEOPLE MANAGEMENT™
(Planning - People - Leadership - Change)

DEFINITION:

Strategic People Planning

Plus

Strategic (Enterprise-Wide) Change

Plus

Leadership and Management

THREE GOALS:

Work On The Enterprise:
#1 Design Clarity of Purpose
(Strategic, Business, and Annual People Plans)

Work In The Enterprise:
#2 Build Simplicity of Execution
(Successful Implementation and Enterprise-Wide Change)

Check On The Enterprise:
#3 Sustain a System of Results
(Annual Strategic Review and Update)

The Results:
People Excellence and Superior Results
(Year After Year)

THREE MAIN PREMISES:

#1 Planning and Change are *the Primary* job of Leadership

#2 "People Support What They Help Create"

#3 Use Systems Thinking
Focus on Outcomes – Serve the Customer

Five Phases of STRATEGIC MANAGEMENT

– Results –

Business Excellence and Superior Results

(Year After Year)

abcsm-people.eps

hrm1.pmd

1420 Monitor Road • San Diego • California • 92110-1545 • (619) 275-6528 • Fax (619) 275-0324

Table of Contents

CREATING THE PEOPLE EDGE

Human resources are probably
the last great cost (investment?)
that is relatively unmanaged
and unreported/measured.

hrm1.pmd

1420 Monitor Road • San Diego • California • 92110-1545 • (619) 275-6528 • Fax (619) 275-0324

PART A
NEW ROLES AND STRUCTURES

EXECUTIVE BRIEFING ON STRATEGIC PEOPLE PLANNING

OFFSITE MEETING — INCLUDING PLAN-TO-PLAN SESSION

Main Purposes: Educating on HRM

1. To gain a common set of principles and knowledge about the **three main premises** for the successful creation of the People Edge.

2. To identify the three goals of Strategic People Planning; to recognize that planning is really one part of a three-part **Strategic Management System** (SMS); to learn what that really means.

3. To understand how to design, build, and sustain (i.e., create) the **"People Edge"** through The Systems Thinking Approach℠.

4. To assess and examine our **Six People Edge Best Practices Areas** research vs. your current organization.

5. To assess and examine all aspects of the **strategic people issues** facing us and our current people edge status as a way to understand the Reinvented Strategic People Planning Model and to determine where we stand in our current planning efforts.

Main Purpose: Organizing and Tailoring

6. To conduct an actual Plan-to-Plan session in order to determine next steps (if any) for a tailored Strategic People Planning process for our organization (and the rest of the Strategic Management System).

Attendees

The Core Planning Team (including all senior management and HR top executives) as a minumum. It can also include other key stakeholders in the morning session as well (Executive Briefing section).

Note

See the next page for a high level overview of The ABCs of a Strategic Management System.

hrm1.pmd

1420 Monitor Road • San Diego • California • 92110-1545 • (619) 275-6528 • Fax (619) 275-0324

THE STATE OF HR: DO OR DIE!

—Lesley Young

It's do or die time for strategic HR. For decades HR has been talking about what it is and how it works. But worldwide failure to execute has dangerously undermined HR's chances of ever becoming business players, shows the industry's most comprehensive study.

Execute or be executed is the resounding prediction of The Human Resources Planning Society 1999 fourth annual international state of the HR industry report.

"Now is the time for HR. Either we blossom or be blown away (because) HR is on the brink of extinction," said Michael Takla, coauthor of the report.

"On the other hand, HR professionals might not have the skills to pull through with what they are asked to so," Takla added.

While all respondents agreed that the two top HR functions for the next five years are improving business-partner skills and linking HR practices with strategy, they gave the current HR functions barely passing grade.

He said the future of HR rests with organizations' top HR professionals. They have to establish credibility, be personable and make contacts with management. "They need to be seen first as a business partner—HR professional second—to be taken seriously at the table."

Takla said establishing a balance between short-term needs and long-term HR strategies is the number one challenge for HR professionals ... To be strategic ... HR has to be on the top of the larger issues as opposed to only offering up knee-jerk responses.

The report also found internal divisions within HR departments over functions is further perpetuating the crisis.

As long as HR talks that talk, it will be hurting itself, he said. "There is always going to be a requirement for HR expertise. But the HR function is going to look a lot different in the future."

He said a lot of HR will be outsourced. "We are already seeing that, especially with recruitment and processing transactions (i.e, payroll)(. I am not predicting extremes ... but the HR function will definitely be shrinking down the road."

Source: *"Dire Future Predicted for Non-Strategic HR Leaders,"* Canadian HR Reporter, October 18, 1999

hrm1.pmd

1420 Monitor Road • San Diego • California • 92110-1545 • (619) 275-6528 • Fax (619) 275-0324

CRITICAL PEOPLE ISSUES LIST

(AND ENVIRONMENTAL PEOPLE TRENDS)

Instructions: Please answer the following questions individually and then discuss as a total group.

#1. What are the 5-10 **Environmental People Trends**—projections—opportunities—threats facing us over the life of our Strategic HR Plan?	#2. What are the 5-10 most important **critical people issues** facing us today as an organization
S Socio-demographics	
K Competition	
E Economics **E** Ecology	
P Political	
T Technical	
I Industry/Substitutes	
C Customer (Internal/External)	

Note: Use this list as the content framework and "grounding" for the strategic HR planning process. Bring it out at the end of the planning process to ensure you've covered these issues/trends adequately.

hrm1.pmd

1420 Monitor Road • San Diego • California • 92110-1545 • (619) 275-6528 • Fax (619) 275-0324

HR Reaching for the 21st Century

By comparing the views of nearly 3,000 professionals, IBM finds a star to steer by.

Concluding that **HR management is in "the throes of a radical transformation,"** the study found that a majority of the respondents see a new HR function taking shape: "Human Resources is being transformed from a specialized, stand-alone function to a broad, corporate competency in which HR and line managers build partnerships to gain competitive advantage and achieve overall business goals."

—Adapted from *HR Magazine*

Leaders and Laggards

Human resources ranked last in a survey of how companies rate their departments' service to internal customers.

According to *Internal Service Performance: What's Happening in American Companies and How To Improve It,* 60 percent of executives responding to the survey said that inferior internal service hobbles their ability to compete effectively.

More than 800 executives responded to the study, conducted jointly by Wm. Schiemann & Associates and *Quality* magazine.

Only 24 percent gave human resources a favorable rating. The quality function earned the best marks—48 percent of respondents rated it favorably.

Respondents who rated their internal services unfavorably cited the following as barriers to change: lack of leadership (77 percent), inappropriate organizational culture (62 percent), lack of perceived need for improvement (61 percent), and ineffective organizational structures (55 percent).

Source: Erica Gordon Sorohan, *"In Practice"*

hrm1.pmd

1420 Monitor Road • San Diego • California • 92110-1545 • (619) 275-6528 • Fax (619) 275-0324

PEOPLE PRACTICES *DO MAKE A DIFFERENCE* IN CORPORATE PERFORMANCE

Companies using the best people practices show **both**
A Higher Degree of Productivity
and Stronger Market Performance

Society for Human Resource Management and CCH Limited Survey

The Research is In:
Employers that score in the top 25% for quality people practices also have superior index ratings for productivity, market value and sales performance.

Do 25% of your workers believe they could accomplish more if you used better management practices?

Identified Barriers to Productivity Include:
* Failure to closely supervise the work (37%)

* Failure to involve employees in decision-making (34%)

* Failure to provide opportunities for advancement or promotion (29%)

* Failure to provide sufficient training (28%)

* Hiring the wrong people (26%)

Moral
Companies investing in employee development enjoy significantly higher market value.

Source: From a survey of 1200 employees conducted for William M. Mercer Ltd.

hrm1.pmd

BECOMING A STRATEGIC PARTNER

TWO BRANCHES OF HUMAN RESOURCES

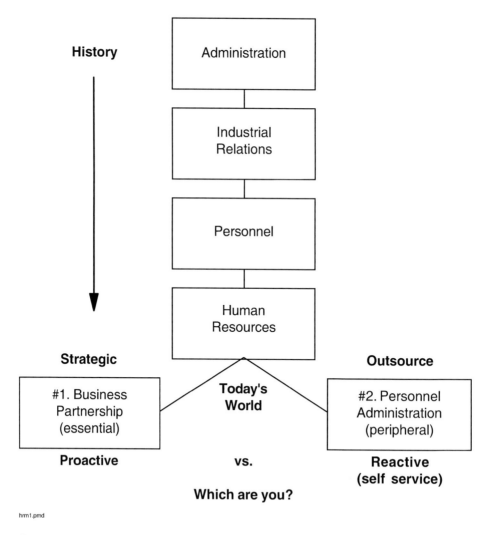

History

Administration

Industrial Relations

Personnel

Human Resources

Today's World

Strategic

#1. Business Partnership (essential)

Proactive

Outsource

#2. Personnel Administration (peripheral)

Reactive (self service)

vs.

Which are you?

hrm1.pmd

1420 Monitor Road • San Diego • California • 92110-1545 • (619) 275-6528 • Fax (619) 275-0324

SOME STRATEGIC PEOPLE TRENDS

—compiled by the Centre

1. **Intellectual Capital**—The attraction and retention of intellectual capital continues to be a challenge. Greater emphasis is being placed on developing people as a critical asset for the organization's future growth and development.

2. **Recruitment Challenges**—One of the greatest challenges facing organizations is actually finding the right people to do the job. The importance of recruitment and selection is increasing and the need to use more innovative ways of recruiting has become a priority.

3. **Performance Management**—Performance Management continues to be important and still needing improvement in guiding performance development and in forming pay decisions. 360° Appraisal Systems are being increasingly utilized. A key performance management challenge is the ability to clearly state and measure employee goals and objectives.

4. **Profitability and Growth**—Organizations will need to continue to increase revenue and reduce costs. The HR function will need to be delivered in a more cost effective way, as well as ensuring the cost effective utilization of organizational resources.

5. **Individual Capability and Organizational Competence**—A key source of organizational competitiveness will be the development of the distinctive competence of the organization, that will allow it to sustain a competitive advantage, along with the specific individual capabilities required by the individuals to deliver it.

    Competency models continue to be used as a means to develop and measure performance.

6. **Globalization**—Organizations continue to grow nationally and internationally, requiring different skills and approaches to manage the organization's customers and staff on a national scale.

7. **Culture Change**—Shaping organizational culture to sustain a competitive culture and reach desired outcomes continues to be a major organizational challenge.

8. **Information Technology**—The growth of technology applications in both HR and organizations continues. This has implications for the overall workforce where there will be a requirement for changing skills to meet the demands of technology, especially as a source of competitive advantage.

    Additionally, HR will need to use the new technology to become more cost efficient and also to enable line managers to carry out their Human Resource responsibilities more easily through 'self-service' concepts, etc.

9. **The Changing Workforce Agenda**—There is an increasing shift regarding the relationship with employees in the workforce. The issue of diminished loyalty to individual employers has been reinforced by the increased emphasis being placed on individuals for their own success. This is placing greater emphasis on the need for managers to develop ways to motivate, reward and recognize employees.

10. **Balancing Work and Personal Life**—Surveys continue to show that employees are working significantly longer hours, and often under greater pressure. The challenge is for employees to be able to effectively balance personal and work time.

hrm1.pmd

1420 Monitor Road • San Diego • California • 92110-1545 • (619) 275-6528 • Fax (619) 275-0324

THE HUMAN RESOURCE FUNCTION—
SOME DIRECTIONS AND CHALLENGES

—compiled by the Centre

1. **Business Partner and Leader**
   The need for the Human Resource Function to become a true business partner and leader with management, in order to meet business and customer needs, will continue to grow.
2. **Strategic Focus**
   The Human Resource Function needs to be able to help in strategically positioning the organization to achieve its business success. At the same time, it will need to be able to execute HR strategy, through the development and implementation of specific HR practices and actions.
3. **An External Focus**
   The need for the Human Resource function to focus on customer, investor and community needs, as well as employees, continues to be a major trend.
4. **Value-Added Approach**
   The Human Resource Function is being increasingly challenged to demonstrate its value added or return on investment approach to the organization. Emphasis is placed on the deliverables rather than the "doables".
5. **HR as a Change Agent**
   HR professionals need to continue to assist in the facilitation of the change process, to ensure the establishment and maintenance of the culture desired to sustain competitive advantage.
6. **HR Staffing Structure and Ratios**
   Staffing ratios for the HR Function have remained the same or continuing to decrease.
   Outsourcing selected Human Resource functions continues and is expected to continue both in the U.S. and internationally. Some key areas of outsourcing include:
   - Employee Assistance Programs
   - Benefits and Pension Administration
   - Recruitment and Selection
   - Organizational/Employee Surveys
   - Training
   - HR Administration
7. **Cost Reduction/Self Service**
   Cost reduction has become a key strategy for Human Resource Practitioners. This occurs through eliminating non-value added work, outsourcing, self service and streamlining the HR Function.
8. **Use of Technology**
   Technology becomes one of the key drivers for streamlining and automation. It also provides a valuable aid in assisting managers to manage their own resources effectively. The increasing use of "service centers" takes advantage of new technology.
9. **Integrating People Practices to Business Direction**
   Maximum impact occurs when people practices are fully integrated with business direction and strategy.
10. **Partnerships**
    The challenge is to establish strong partnerships not only with managers but customers and shareholders alike in the management of the HR Function.

hrm1.pmd

1420 Monitor Road • San Diego • California • 92110-1545 • (619) 275-6528 • Fax (619) 275-0324

SECTION II
MANAGEMENT ROLES ARE CHANGING

ORGANIZATIONAL ROLES FOR
THE IDEAL PEOPLE EDGE

DEFINITION

The process of identifying the respective value adding roles of employees, management and Human Resources staff in contributing to the business success of the organization.

> "Best Practice" Human Resource Research emphasizes the importance of HR partnering with Line Management to develop and implement high impact people management results.
>
> Line Management accountability in the implementation of people management practices is also a key best practice indicator.

FOUR PEOPLE EDGE ROLES

- Strategic Partner
- Consultant/Trainer (Facilitator)
- Coach/Advisor

- Policy/Direction
- Visible Leadership
- Responsible/Accountable

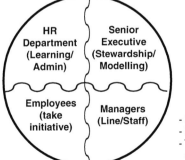

- Self management
- Self service
- Empowerment

- Manage people issues
- Lead/Develop people
- Trainer - Coach - Facilitator - conflict resolver

hrm2.pmd

1420 Monitor Road • San Diego • California • 92110-1545 • (619) 275-6528 • Fax (619) 275-0324

KEY PEOPLE EDGE ROLES
(IN AN ORGANIZATION)

HR Department

1.

2.

3.

4.

5.

6.

Senior Executives

1.

2.

3.

4.

5.

6.

Employees

1.

2.

3.

4.

5.

6.

Managers

1.

2.

3.

4.

5.

6.

hrm2.pmd

1420 Monitor Road • San Diego • California • 92110-1545 • (619) 275-6528 • Fax (619) 275-0324

SECTION III
EXECUTIVE DEVELOPMENT BOARD

EXECUTIVE/EMPLOYEE DEVELOPMENT BOARD (EDB) CONCEPT

> ## "Invest in Your People First"

The people management practices of any organization should be viewed as a system of people flow from hiring, through their careers, and through retirement and/or termination. See the Centre's copyrighted HR Systems Model and assessment tools. Making this all happen is the responsibility of senior management; usually best done through an "EDB" (Executive/Employee Development Board) focused solely on this framework and "creating people as a competitive business advantage." *(The "People Edge")*

For example: As a Board, this reinforces senior management's responsibility to carry out your "stewardship" responsibilities towards yourselves and the rest of your employees. The best way to explain this fully is example (on the next page) from the author's days as an Executive Vice President of Imperial Corporation of America (ICA), a $14 billion financial services company formerly in San Diego, California.

In essence, this Executive Stewardship Board is responsible for the Human Resource Management flow and continuity. It is executive responsibility to link staffing to business strategy via:

- hiring
- selection (up/lateral)
- succession planning/core competencies
- developmental jobs/experiences
- Leadership Development System
- training: classroom (internal, external)

- organization design/structure
- socio-demographic trends
- employee surveys of satisfaction/360º feedback
- rewards/performance system
- workforce planning

A mechanism/structure of how to achieve management continuity is needed (i.e., a linking pin of Boards):

1. Executive Development Board (EDB)—executive team
2. Management Development Board (MDB)—all department heads/teams
3. Employee Development Committees (EEDC)—all supervisors/section head areas

The desired outcomes include:

Right person — Right job — Right time — Right organization — Right skills!

Sample Monthly Executive Meetings

Week 1	Operational/Business Issues
Week 2	Strategic Planning and Change Process/Status
Week 3	Strategic Change Issues
Week 4	Customer Satisfaction
***Week 5**	Executive/Employee Development Board (EDB)
(Quarterly)	Staff, promotion, succession, development
	– HR Executive as secretary to Senior Management

hrm3.pmd

1420 Monitor Road • San Diego • California • 92110-1545 • (619) 275-6528 • Fax (619) 275-0324

EXECUTIVE/EMPLOYEE DEVELOPMENT BOARDS (EDB)

1. **Purpose:** To proactively manage and create the organization's People Edge

2. **Number of EDBs:** Using the linking pin concept.

   I. 1st level
      "Executive EDB"

   II. 2nd level
      4 "SVP EDBs"

   III. 3rd level
      14 "Management EDBs"

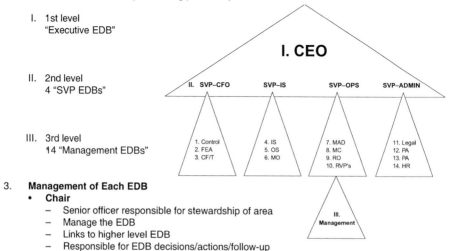

3. **Management of Each EDB**
   - **Chair**
     - Senior officer responsible for stewardship of area
     - Manage the EDB
     - Links to higher level EDB
     - Responsible for EDB decisions/actions/follow-up

   - **Members**
     - Direct reports of each Chair
     - Responsible for succession presentations
     - Must wear a corporate hat in the meetings for them to be successful
     - Represent their employees as well

   - **Secretary/HR Rep**
     - Provides content input
     - Ensures employee fair treatment
     - Handles minutes and logistics
     - Ensures process properly occurs as desired
     - Is the linkage person laterally to EDBs
     - Provide follow-up continually on EDB desired actions

4. **Meetings:** As necessary but initially quarterly or monthly depending on rollout of tasks.

5. **Rollout:** Recommend initially that only Executive EDB and SVP EDBs (4) be established so that officers can gain experience with process prior to involving Directors in 14 officer areas.

hrm3.pmd

1420 Monitor Road • San Diego • California • 92110-1545 • (619) 275-6528 • Fax (619) 275-0324

EXECUTIVE/EMPLOYEE DEVELOPMENT BOARD PROCESS

Step 1: Chairman forms EDB and holds first organizational meeting.
- Timing/Agenda is set for first year
- Briefing/understanding of entire EDB concept is completed

Step 2: Conduct Strategic People Plan for the organization during the People Planning. Each member can put goals on the agenda for their area of responsibility. Sample ones might be any of the following:
- reducing turnover to 17%
- succession planning
- executive development
- management development
- department transfers (corporate assets)
- careers at the organization
  - Career Management System
  - career ladders
  - for professionals/for managers
- Performance Management System
  - goals/coaching
  - appraisals/careers
- organizational reward systems/pay for performance
- core people competencies needed for future
- recognition programs
- hiring profile for organization/recruiting and selection system
- employee expectations (psychological contract)

Step 3: Once succession planning is desired to be a part of the EDB agenda:
- The Succession/Career Management System must be completely understood.
- Appropriate training must be undertaken to ensure managers are coaches on careers.

Step 4: Actual EDB succession planning process:
1. Follow steps 1-4 above to prepare for succession planning.
2. All candidates will need to fill out our Career Development forms.
3. Managers fill out their Performance Appraisals.
4. Each member present their succession plans for their position (may also do it for next level).
5. Review/critique plan/candidate by entire EDB.
6. EDB make decisions/recommendations on each plan/candidate's development.
7. HR representative take good notes/summarize discussion for future use.
8. HR Rep issue confidential minutes.
9. Each member provides feedback to candidate/personnel as appropriate for their development.
10. Each member take specific action as directed by EDB with HR assistance.
11. EDB follow-up semiannually as to results achieved by each member and their candidates.
12. EDBs update succession plans yearly.
13. EDBs implement plans as appropriate succession needs arise.
14. HR Rep provides linkage/input to other EDBs as appropriate to ensure interdepartmental/cross-functional considerations are a part of all EDB decisions (eliminate stove pipe careers).

hrm3.pmd

1420 Monitor Road • San Diego • California • 92110-1545 • (619) 275-6528 • Fax (619) 275-0324

THE EMPLOYEE DEVELOPMENT COMMITTEE (EDC)

"Our Commitment to Our Employees"

What's the purpose of the Employee Development Committee (EDC)?

It serves as a forum to carry our employee stewardship responsibilities. We realize that our success and profitability come from the strength and capabilities of *all* of our employees.

This committee's only purpose is to discuss and decide on human resources issues, policies and programs so that we can continue to "grow" the talent we have in the organization and make ICA a great company in which to work, learn and develop.

This EDC provides a direct link to the Personnel Committee of the Board of Directors, ensuring that sound investment in our human resources remains a corporate priority.

What are the goals of the EDC?

Simply stated, the goals of the EDC are to effectively carry out the following ICA Management Principles:

3. Achieve and reward outstanding performance.
   Also confront and correct poor performance.
5. Use human and financial resources wisely in support of the corporate direction.
9. Involve our employees by providing opportunities to contribute.
10. Develop productive employees. Delegate, train and motivate employees to their maximum potential.

The EDC philosophy sounds good. But how will this translate into action?

Some of the employee benefit programs and development concepts that have come out of EDC meetings include:

• Shared Savings Plan – 401(k)

• Employee banking program enhancements

• Employee Pension & Benefits program changes/enhancements

• Performance management sysutem and the rewards for performance concept

• Team and individual non-financial rewards, recognition and incentives

• Merit increase programs and plans

• Career development and succession planning commencing with executive level assessment and slated to progress through the entire organization in later years

• Training and development program for managers/supervisors in:

   – Performance Planning & Review

   – Goal Setting

   – Coaching & Counseling

   ...to name a few

Who is a member of the Employee Development Committee?

Chairman:
President & CEO

Members:
Exec. V.P., Retail Banking
Senior V.P., Legal
Exec. V.P., Administration
Exec. V.P., Mortgage Banking
Exec. V.P., Finance
Exec. V.P., Corporate Information Systems

Secretary:
Sr. V.P., Human Resources

This committee is supported by an implementation team from the following departments:

Benefits
Communications
Employee Relations
Employment
Training & Development

When does the EDC meet?

Quarterly, or more often, if necessary.

How do I find out what the committee is doing for us?

Primarily through articles in "Inside ICA" and other employee publications. We want to inform you on an on-going basis that much time, effort and attention is being spent on you – to help you develop and grow as you contribute to the success of the ICA team.

hrm3.pmd

1420 Monitor Road • San Diego • California • 92110-1545 • (619) 275-6528 • Fax (619) 275-0324

EXECUTIVE/EMPLOYEE DEVELOPMENT BOARD

Instructions: Establish an "Executive/Employee Development Board" (EDB) to manage the planning succession and development of the people in the organization to create "The People Edge."

Establish an Executive/Employee Development Board (EDB)

1. Purpose

2. Goals

3. Membership

4. Meeting Frequency

5. Communications Methods

6. Secretary/Assistant

hrm3.pmd

1420 Monitor Road • San Diego • California • 92110-1545 • (619) 275-6528 • Fax (619) 275-0324

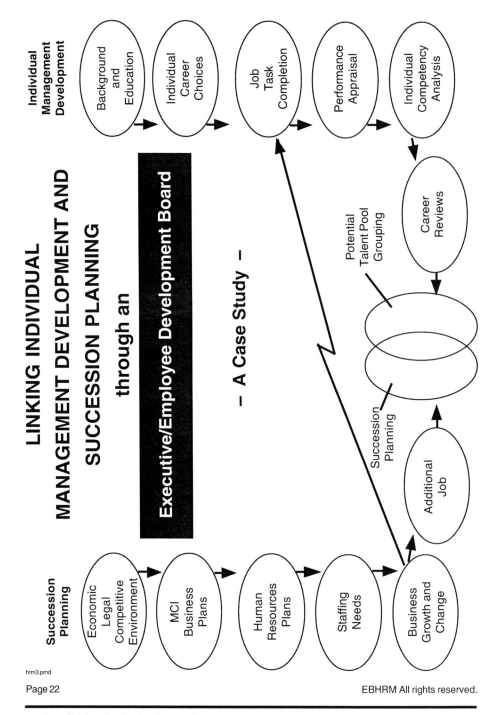

LINKING INDIVIDUAL MANAGEMENT DEVELOPMENT AND SUCCESSION PLANNING

through an

Executive/Employee Development Board

– A Case Study –

Individual Management Development

- Background and Education
- Individual Career Choices
- Job Task Completion
- Performance Appraisal
- Individual Competency Analysis
- Career Reviews

Succession Planning

- Economic Legal Competitive Environment
- MCI Business Plans
- Human Resources Plans
- Staffing Needs
- Business Growth and Change

Potential Talent Pool Grouping

Succession Planning

Additional Job

1420 Monitor Road • San Diego • California • 92110-1545 • (619) 275-6528 • Fax (619) 275-0324

PART B
THE SYSTEM

SECTION IV
STRATEGIC PEOPLE PLANNING OVERVIEW

DIFFERENCES BETWEEN ORGANIZATIONAL PEOPLE PLANS AND DIVISION HR PLANS

	Systems Thinking	Analytical Thinking
Dimensions	**Organizational People Plan**	**Divisional HR Plan**
Purpose	Translating business strategies first into organizational capabilities and then into HR practices.	Building a strategy, organization and action plan focused on making the HR function or department more effective.
Owner	Line Managers	HR Executives
Measures	Business results through use of HR practices	Effectiveness and efficiency of the HR practices
Audience	• Managers who use HR practices for business results • Employees who are affected by HR practices • Customers who receive the benefits of effective organizations • Investors who reap the rewards of organization capabilities	• HR professionals who design and deliver HR practices • Line managers who use HR practices
Roles	• Line managers as owner • HR professional as facilitator	• Line manager as investor • HR professional as creator

Adapted from D. Ulrich, *"Human Resource Champions"*

hrm4.pmd

1420 Monitor Road • San Diego • California • 92110-1545 • (619) 275-6528 • Fax (619) 275-0324

ANALYTIC VS. SYSTEMS THINKING
(Strategic Consistency yet Operational Flexibility)

(Outside – In – Outside Again: Both Are Then Useful)

 Success Key: *Organizational Systems Fit, Alignment, and Integrity*

Analytic Thinking (Analysis of Today)	vs.	Systems Thinking (Synthesis for the Future)
1. We/they	vs.	1. Customers/stakeholders
2. Independent	vs.	2. Interdependent
3. Activities/tasks/means	and	3. Outcomes/ends
4. Problem solving	and	4. Solution seeking
5. Today is fine	vs.	5. Shared vision of future
6. Units/departments	and	6. Total organization
7. Silo mentality	vs.	7. Cross-functional teamwork
8. Closed environment	vs.	8. Openness and feedback
9. Department goals	and	9. Shared core strategies
10. Strategic Planning project	vs.	10. Strategic Management System
11. Hierarchy and controls	and	11. Serve the customer
12. Not my job	vs.	12. Communications and collaboration
13. Isolated change	vs.	13. Systemic change
14. Linear/begin-end	vs.	14. Circular/repeat cycles
15. Little picture/view	vs.	15. Big picture/holistic perspective
16. Short-term	and	16. Long-term
17. Separate issues	vs.	17. Related issues
18. Symptoms	and	18. Root causes
19. Isolated Events	and	19. Patterns/trends
20. Activities/Actions	and	20. Clear outcome expectations (Goals/Values)
Sum: Parts are Primary	**vs.**	**Whole is Primary**

 Using "Analytic Approaches to Systems Problems"

Systems vs. Analytic Thinking

In Systems Thinking —the whole is primary and the parts are secondary

vs.

In Analytic Thinking—the parts are primary and the whole is secondary.

hrm4.pmd

1420 Monitor Road • San Diego • California • 92110-1545 • (619) 275-6528 • Fax (619) 275-0324

SYSTEMS THINKING—PARADIGM SHIFTS

Obsolescence

...as a result of the current paradigm shift, the standard way of doing business is rapidly becoming obsolete and irrelevant.

"From → To"

Old-Fashioned Industrial Age Concepts →	**New Systems Age Concepts**
Bureaucracy/Functions	Network and Integration
Focus on Institution	Focus on Individuals/Teams
Control	Empowerment
Structure	Flexibility/Minimum Hierarchy
Stability	Change
Self-Sufficiency	Interdependencies
Directive Management	Inspirational Leadership/Vision Shared
Affordable Quality	Value-Added
Personal Security	Personal Growth
Title, Rank, Compensation	Making a Difference
To Compete	To Build and Sustain
Domestic	Global/World Village
Vertical Integration	Alliances/Collaborations
Economy of Scale	Economy of Speed
Single Loop Learning	Double-Loop Learning

Our Level of Thinking

Problems that are created
by our current level of thinking
can't be solved
by that same level of thinking.

—Albert Einstein

hrm4.pmd

1420 Monitor Road • San Diego • California • 92110-1545 • (619) 275-6528 • Fax (619) 275-0324

SYSTEMS THINKING:
"A NEW ORIENTATION TO LIFE"

"From Complexity to Simplicity"

Systems: Systems are made up of a set of components that work together for the overall objective of the whole (output).

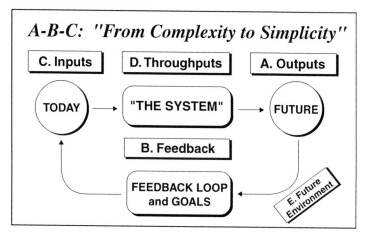

Five Questions in Sequence

| A | Where do we want to be? (i.e., our ends, outcomes, purposes, goals, holistic vision |

| B | How will we know when we get there? (i.e., the customers' needs and wants connected into a quantifiable feedback system) |

| C | Where are we now? (i.e., today's issues and problems) |

| D | How do we get there? (i.e., close the gap from C → A in a complete holistic way) |

| E | ongoing: What will/may change in your environment in the future? |

vs. Analytic Thinking *Which:*

1. Starts with today and the current state, issues, and problems.
2. Breaks the issues and/or problems into their smallest components.
3. Solves each component separately (i.e., maximizes the solution).
4. Has no far reaching vision or goal (just the absence of the problem).

Note: In systems thinking, the whole is primary and the parts are secondary (not vice-versa).

hrm4.pmd

"If you don't know where you're going, any road will get you there."

1420 Monitor Road • San Diego • California • 92110-1545 • (619) 275-6528 • Fax (619) 275-0324

STRATEGIC HUMAN RESOURCE/PEOPLE MANAGEMENT SYSTEM (AND NEEDS ASSESSMENT)

System	Step: Needs (H-M-L)	Definition
	___1. Planning to Plan	The pre-work to the planning process that is required to determine organizational readiness; who needs to be involved in the planning to ensure ownership and the identification of strategic information that needs to be gathered to assist in the planning process. Form the Planning Team (Employee Development Board), get educated, organized and tailor the process to your needs.
E Environ- ment	2. Business Scanning Process	
	___ • Corporate Strategic Direction	Identification of the corporation's key strategies and directions, and people related business issues implications.
	___ • Organizational Values	Identification of the core values of the corporation and the analysis of the related people management implications.
	___ • Stakeholder Expectations	The identification of stakeholders (who impact or are impacted by the plan) and an analysis of their expectations of the Strategic Human Resource Plan
	___ • Environmental Scan	Scanning and analysis of the impact of the following areas in the development of the plan. *Note:* Discuss the total environment, **not** just the people side. S Social – People K Competition E Economics/Environment P Political T Technological I Industry C Customer
A Outcomes	3. Ideal People Edge (for business success)	
	• People Vision	An inspirational statement of where the Organization wants to be positioned in the future in relation to people management for competitive advantage.
	___ • HR Dept. Mission	An outline of why the HR Function exists, its purpose and who it serves—i.e., its core business and value added.
	___ • Organization Roles	The respective roles that employees, management, customers and HR play in the contribution of people management strategies to organizational success.
	___ • Future Competencies	The distinctive people related competencies that will ensure the success of the organization.

hrm4.pmd

continued

1420 Monitor Road • San Diego • California • 92110-1545 • (619) 275-6528 • Fax (619) 275-0324

STRATEGIC HUMAN RESOURCE/PEOPLE MANAGEMENT SYSTEM (AND NEEDS ASSESSMENT)

System	Step: Needs (H-M-L)	Definition
B **Feedback**	___ 4. **Key People Success Success Measures**	The establishment of the high level quantifiable measures that will be used to determine HR success in adding value to the organization for employees, customers, shareholders and community.
C **Inputs**	___ 5. **Assessment of Current People Practices**	The assessment of current people practices against the key Best Practice HR leverage points as a basis for determining strategy development.
	6. **Developing People Strategies**	
	___ • Alignment of Delivery	The development of core people management strategies that are aligned to the business delivery needs of the customer.
	___ • Attunement of People	Development of people management strategies that will attune the hearts and minds of employees to the vision and culture of the organization.
	___ 7. **3-Year People Edge Plan**	The development of a plan that outlines the key activities of the next three years to achieve the people edge vision of the organization.
	___ • 1-Year Department Operational Plan and Budgets	The specific actions that will occur over a twelve month period, in response to the critical priorities established (for the 12 month planning period) in the people-edge plan.
	___ 8. **Plan to Implement**	The development of a plan to ensure the effective implementation of the Strategic HR Plan.
D **Processes**	___ 9. **Strategy Implementation and Change**	The development and implementation of specific strategies that will ensure the required implementation and change.
	___ 10. **Annual People Review & Update**	The regular monitoring and yearly review of the plan to: • celebrate achievements • ensure targets have been reached • establish new priorities and action plans
	___ **Parallel Involvement Process**	A framework for engaging key stakeholders who impact or are impacted by the strategic human resource planning process. It ensures their ownership of the process and involvement at all stages of the planning/implementation process.

hrm4.pmd

1420 Monitor Road • San Diego • California • 92110-1545 • (619) 275-6528 • Fax (619) 275-0324

YEARLY STRATEGIC PEOPLE MANAGEMENT CYCLE
THE SYSTEMS THINKING APPROACH™

"CREATING PEOPLE AS YOUR COMPETITIVE BUSINESS ADVANTAGE"

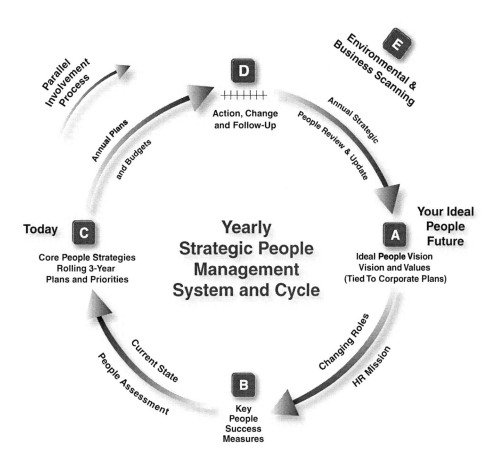

E Environmental & Business Scanning

Parallel Involvement Process

Annual Plans and Budgets

D Action, Change and Follow-Up

Annual Strategic People Review & Update

Your Ideal People Future
A Ideal People Vision
Vision and Values
(Tied To Corporate Plans)

Today
C Core People Strategies
Rolling 3-Year
Plans and Priorities

Yearly
Strategic People
Management
System and Cycle

Changing Roles
HR Mission

Current State
People Assessment

B Key
People
Success
Measures

"Thinking Backwards To Your Future"
The Systems Thinking Approach™

MCPE-02_2

hrm4.pmd

1420 Monitor Road • San Diego • California • 92110-1545 • (619) 275-6528 • Fax (619) 275-0324

COMMON MISTAKES IN STRATEGIC PEOPLE PLANNING

Instructions: Place a check if these apply or might apply to you.

_____ 1. Not even doing a formal people planning process.

_____ 2. Failing to integrate Strategic Human Resource Planning at all levels.

_____ 3. Delegating Strategic Human Resource Planning to the HR function only.

_____ 4. Keeping HR Planning separate from day-to-day management.

_____ 5. Conducting long-range forecasting only.

_____ 6. Having a scattershot approach to Strategic HR Planning.

_____ 7. Developing vision, mission and value statements as fluff.

_____ 8. Failing to use strategic information and analysis to drive the plan.

_____ 9. Failing to take into account the needs of all key stakeholders—employees, customers and investors.

_____10. Failing to identify the critical business issues and competency requirements as a basis for driving the strategic plan.

_____11. Failing to set up/complete an effective implementation process.

_____12. Conducting business as usual after Strategic Human Resource Planning (SPOTS Syndrome).

_____13. Not having line management lead in the development of the plan.

_____14. Lacking a scoreboard: Measuring what's easy, not what's important.

_____15. Lacking a balanced scoreboard approach—i.e., measuring financial, customer, business process and employee measures.

_____16. Neglecting to benchmark yourself against the competition.

_____17. Seeing the planning document as an end in itself.

_____18. Trying to facilitate the process yourself.

_____19. Violating the *"people support what they help create"* syndrome.

_____20. Failure to identify the "key leverage points" that will result in the greatest strategic change.

_____21. Failure to integrate strategies in the implementation process.

_____22. Failing to make the "tough people choices."

hrm4.pmd

1420 Monitor Road • San Diego • California • 92110-1545 • (619) 275-6528 • Fax (619) 275-0324

SECTION V
STRATEGIC PEOPLE PLANNING
(Step-by-Step)

STEP 1: PLAN-TO-PLAN

"PEOPLE SUPPORT WHAT THEY HELP CREATE"

Question: Which tasks do we need to do as part of Step #1?

Task

1. Organization Specifications Sheet
2. A High Performance Organization Mini Survey
3. Pre-Work Strategic Planning Briefing Questionnaire
4. Executive Briefing on Strategic HR Planning
5. Personal Readiness/Experiences in Strategic HR Planning
6. Strategic HR Planning Process (past Levels of Effectiveness)
7. Readiness Steps and Actions (barriers and issues)
8. Organizational Fact Sheet For Strategic HR Planning
9. Strategic People Issues List
10. Strategic HR Planning Team Formed and Staff Support Team identified
11. Executive/Employee Development Board (EDB) Membership Formed (May also be the Planning Team, or a subset of it)
12. Identification of Key Stakeholders

Task

13. Key Stakeholder Involvement
14. Initial Environmental Scanning/Current State Assessment Required
15. Reinvented Strategic HR Planning Model (tailored to our needs)
16. Strategic HR Planning Link (to budgets)
17. Leadership Development Skills (organizational and individual self-change/training needed)
18. Individual Commitment to Strategic Management Must Be High (not just Strategic Planning)
19. Organizational Commitment (Strategic Implementation and Change)
20. Strategic HR Planning Updates Communicated to Others
21. Energizers Needed (for our meetings)
22. Strategic HR Planning Meeting (process observer for team building)
23. Action Minutes (format to use)
24. Meeting Processing (guide to use)
25. Meeting Closure-Action Planning Checklist (at end of each mtg.)

Note: This EB Notebook does not include all the tasks. For complete task information, refer to Workbook #1—*Plan-to-Plan*.

hrm5.pmd

1420 Monitor Road • San Diego • California • 92110-1545 • (619) 275-6528 • Fax (619) 275-0324

KEY INFORMATION TO BE GATHERED FOR THE STRATEGIC HR PLANNING PROCESS

- Annual Report
  - Staffing numbers, financial data, etc.

- Business Initiatives
  - Key directions not included in corporate or business plans

- Key Human Resource Planning and Staffing Information
  i.e.,
  - Turnover rates
  - Absenteeism
  - Occupational health and safety complaints
  - Training expenditure
  - Human resource planning
  - Staff survey data

- Corporate Strategic Plan
  - Organizational mission, values, SWOT, directions and strategies

- Organizational Business Plans
  - Action plans

- Stakeholder Analysis
  - CEO
  - Executive
  - Central agencies
  - Other business units
  - Staff
  - Customer survey data
  - Complaints register, etc.

Some Practical Plan-to-Plan Hints

1. Ensure there is Chief Executive Officer and Senior Management commitment to the planning process—it is critical to its success.

2. Strategic Planning takes time. Make sure that the planning group is aware of the significant time commitment—particularly if consulation is involved.

3. Ensure that the planning team is educated in the planning process before the formal aspects of the planning process commences—it saves time in the long run and provides a better product.

4. Ensure all information and data requirements are identified beforehand; again it saves time in the long run and ensures a better product.

5. Link the Strategic Planning process into the budget cycle as soon as possible. (This may not be possible in the first year of the planning process and may take two years to synchronize.)

6. Ensure staff and other key stakeholders are consulted before the planning process commences; during the planning process and upon its completion. This can involve putting out strategic updates after each meeting, and placing the draft strategic planning document out for comment.

7. Select a comfortable venue, with lots of space and whiteboards—and away from distractions. The venue influences the planning process.

hrm5.pmd

1420 Monitor Road • San Diego • California • 92110-1545 • (619) 275-6528 • Fax (619) 275-0324

STRATEGIC PEOPLE PLANNING "STAFF SUPPORT TEAM"

List Staff Support Team Names:

Position	Typical Tasks	Name
1. Planning	• Strategic/Annual Planning • Business Planning • Current State Assessment	
2. Finance	• Key People Sucess Measures • Budgeting • Current State Assessment	
3. Human Resources	• Performance/Rewards Mgmt. • Training and Development	
4. Communications	• Updates After Each Meeting • Print Final Plan/Plaques • Rollout Plan	
5. Administrative Assistant	• Logistics/Follow-up • Laptop Mintues/Document Revisions • Drafts Strategic Plan	
6. Internal Coordinator **Coordinates** or does 1-7 themselves	**Minimum List** • Parallel Involvement Process • Internal Facilitator • Coordinates Entire Process • Facilitates/Supports the Change Steering Committee • Teach Org. About This	
7. External Consultant	• Facilitates Planning/Change Teams • Develops Internal Coordinator • Devil's Advocate/Tough Choices • Advisor on all Planning/Change	

hrm5.pmd

1420 Monitor Road • San Diego • California • 92110-1545 • (619) 275-6528 • Fax (619) 275-0324

PARALLEL PROCESS

(INSTEAD OF D.A.D.: Decide, Announce, Defend)

SET UP THE PLANNING COMMUNITY

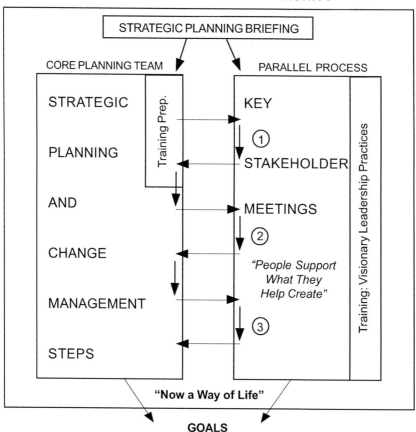

"Now a Way of Life"

GOALS

#1 OWNERSHIP FOR IMPLEMENTATION
#2 BEST POSSIBLE DECISION ON FUTURE VISION

hrm5.pmd

1420 Monitor Road • San Diego • California • 92110-1545 • (619) 275-6528 • Fax (619) 275-0324

PARALLEL INVOLVEMENT PROCESS MEETINGS

PURPOSE (AND AGENDA)

1. To explain the strategic planning effort and your role/involvement in it.
2. To understand the draft documents clearly.
3. To give us input and feedback to take back to the full core planning team
   - Guarantee: Your feedback will be seriously considered.
   - Limitation: Input is being gathered from many different peole. Therefore, it is impossible for each person's input to be automatically placed in the final document exactly as desired.

OVERALL MEETING PURPOSE

1. This is an information sharing and input/feedback meeting.
2. It is not a decision-making meeting. This will be done by the Core Planning Team at their next meeting, based on your feedback.

THE "MAGIC" IS IN THE ITERATION

How to get the best answers?

1. **Creativity comes from:**
   - intense dialogue/thought
   - time to get away/reflect—doing your day-to-day job
   - a second or even third intense dialogue
     - in the Parallel Process
     - in the next planning meeting

2. **Testing via the Parallel Process is the crucible to:**
   - improve the quality of the answers
   - develop "buy in" and commitment to the answer

The Question is—*When are you "ready" for closure?*

hrm5.pmd

1420 Monitor Road • San Diego • California • 92110-1545 • (619) 275-6528 • Fax (619) 275-0324

STEP 2: BUSINESS SCANNING

Definition

The overall scanning and analysis of the environment to ensure strategic, business and people related business issues are identified.

The four components of the Scanning Process:

1. Corporate Strategic Direction — Corporate Strategic Plan (if available)

2. Core Organizational Values — Adopt from the Corporate Strategic Plan

3. Stakeholder Expectations

4. Environmental Scan

> Successful Strategic HR Planning requires an understanding of the strategic direction of the corporation and the critical competencies required to sustain competitive advantage. This then provides the basis to develop high impact people management capabilities to deliver the competencies.

Questions: What do we need to do regarding Step #2?

hrm5.pmd

1420 Monitor Road • San Diego • California • 92110-1545 • (619) 275-6528 • Fax (619) 275-0324

STEP 3:
IDENTIFYING THE IDEAL PEOPLE EDGE

(FOR BUSINESS SUCCESS)

Key Components

- People Vision

- HR Department Mission

- Organizational Roles—4 Different Ones

- Future People Competencies Needed

> Our starting premises are simple: Competition for the future is competition to create and dominate emerging opportunities—to stake out new competitive space. Creating the future is more challenging than playing catch up, in that you have to create your own road map. The goal is not simply to benchmark our competitor's products and processes and imitate its methods, but to develop an independent point of view about tomorrow's opportunities and how to exploit them. Pathbreaking is a lot more rewarding than benchmarking. One doesn't get to the future first by letting someone else blaze the trail.
>
> *Competing for the Future,*
> Hamel & Prahalad

Questions: What do we need to do regarding Step #3?

hrm5.pmd

1420 Monitor Road • San Diego • California • 92110-1545 • (619) 275-6528 • Fax (619) 275-0324

VISION

DEFINITION

The vision is a statement of where the organization wishes to be in the future, and in broad terms what it will achieve for its workforce and the people management.

It should:
- be inspirational
- be challenging
- reflect the changing and challenging nature of Strategic Human Resource Management
- respond to the expectations of stakeholders
- support the strategic direction of the organization

Exercise: Describe below your people edge vision for the organization.

hrm5.pmd

1420 Monitor Road • San Diego • California • 92110-1545 • (619) 275-6528 • Fax (619) 275-0324

MISSION DEVELOPMENT TRIANGLE EXERCISE (HR DEPARTMENT)

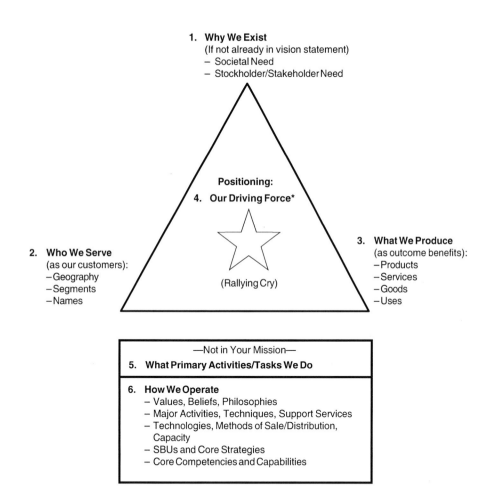

1. **Why We Exist**
   (If not already in vision statement)
   – Societal Need
   – Stockholder/Stakeholder Need

Positioning:

4. **Our Driving Force***

(Rallying Cry)

2. **Who We Serve**
   (as our customers):
   –Geography
   –Segments
   –Names

3. **What We Produce**
   (as outcome benefits):
   –Products
   –Services
   –Goods
   –Uses

—Not in Your Mission—

5. **What Primary Activities/Tasks We Do**

6. **How We Operate**
   – Values, Beliefs, Philosophies
   – Major Activities, Techniques, Support Services
   – Technologies, Methods of Sale/Distribution, Capacity
   – SBUs and Core Strategies
   – Core Competencies and Capabilities

*Note: Your Driving Force can be either a who, a what, a why, or a how (1-2-3-5-6), but it must position you in the organization marketplace differently from your competitors/other functions.

hrm5.pmd

1420 Monitor Road • San Diego • California • 92110-1545 • (619) 275-6528 • Fax (619) 275-0324

DETERMINING FUTURE PEOPLE RELATED COMPETENCIES/CAPABILITIES

DEFINITION

The knowledge, skills (or capabilities that are required organization-wide of individuals to achieve or successfully implement business strategy.

TASK

Building upon our business scan, what are the critical **competencies/capabilities** that we need to develop in our workforce, to reach our people edge vision?

1.

2.

3.

4.

5.

hrm5.pmd

1420 Monitor Road • San Diego • California • 92110-1545 • (619) 275-6528 • Fax (619) 275-0324

STEP 4:
KEY PEOPLE SUCCESS MEASURES DEFINED

Key People Success Measures are the quantifiable outcome measurements of success in achieving the ideal "people edge" on a year-by-year basis to ensure continual improvement towards achieving the ideal future vision.

i.e.,
1. How do you know if you're being successful?
2. How do you know if you're going to get into trouble?
3. Now, if you are off course (in trouble), what corrective actions do you need to take to get the organization back on track to achieve your ideal future vision?

HR Key Success Factors may be either developed for the HR Division itself, and/or for the organization as a whole.

Some Sample People Measures:
1. Recruiting, hiring, workforce planning success/speed
2. Employee satisfaction (survey vs. values)
3. Compensation and evaluation information/number recognition awards
4. Development and succession readiness/backups
5. Turnover costs and rates, wrongful discharge numbers
6. Absenteeism rates, overtime amounts, temp usage

FEEDBACK LOOP
Key People Success Measures
(To Sustain a Competitive Business Advantage Over the Long Term)

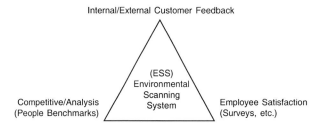

hrm5.pmd

1420 Monitor Road • San Diego • California • 92110-1545 • (619) 275-6528 • Fax (619) 275-0324

KEY PEOPLE SUCCESS MEASURES

ESTIMATED EXCESS CORPORATE COSTS SUMMARY

All costs shown below are projected, annual figures for costs to the Corporation that are considered excessive due to factors which are in the control of managers and employees. This summary has been compiled in order to bring to light the magnitude of potential savings for potentially simple changes in behavior. These numbers are all presented in further detail within the detailed report attached.

		Direct	**Indirect**
1.	Cost overrunns for exceeding salary budgets	$1,392,000.	
2.	Cost of incorrect/late payroll/personnel paperwork	$78,783.	
3.	Cost of staff time on commission plan exceptions	$87,850.	
4.	Cost of exceptions above authorized amounts on commissions	$778,124.	
5.	Cost of non-cumulative draws not offset by commissions	$578,000.	
6.	Cost of benefits paid by company due to functionally stressed employees (employee burnout)	TBD	
7.	Cost of retirement supplements paid to retirees allowed to retire rather than being confronted to correct performance problems	$39,432.	
8.	Annual average termination costs		$3,954,618.
9.	Cost of voluntary turnover with replacement employees hired		$13,275,600.
10.	Cost of "no shows" for internal training programs	$16,000.	
	SUBTOTALS	$2,970,189.	$17,330.218.

Projected Annual Total Excess People Mgmt. Costs $20,300,407.

hrm5.pmd

1420 Monitor Road • San Diego • California • 92110-1545 • (619) 275-6528 • Fax (619) 275-0324

TEN KEY HUMAN CAPITAL METRICS

1. **Revenue Factor** =
$$\frac{\text{Revenue}}{\text{Total FTE}}$$

The basic measure understood by managers. The FTE number should include regular employees and contingent labor.

2. **Voluntary Separation Rate** =
$$\frac{\text{Voluntary Separations}}{\text{Headcount}}$$

Along with the time to fill jobs, this represents potential lost opportunity, lost revenue and more highly stressed employees who have to fill in for departed colleagues.

3. **Human Capital Value** =
$$\frac{\text{Revenue} - (\text{Operating expense} - [\text{Compensation cost} + \text{Benefit cost*}])}{\text{Total FTE}}$$

This is the prime measure of people's contributions in an organization. It answers the question, what are people worth?

4. **Human Capital ROI** =
$$\frac{\text{Revenue} - (\text{Operating expense} - [\text{Compensation cost} + \text{Benefit cost*}])}{(\text{Compensation cost} - \text{Benefit cost})}$$

This is a ratio of dollars spent on pay and benefits to an adjusted profit figure.

5. **Total Compensation Revenue Percent** =
$$\frac{\text{Compensation cost} + \text{Benefit cost}}{\text{Revenue}}$$

If you monitor pay and benefits in comparison to revenue per employee, you can see the return on your investment.

6. **Total Labor Cost Revenue Percent** =
$$\frac{\text{Compensation cost} + \text{Benefit cost} + \text{Other labor cost}}{\text{Revenue}}$$

By looking at total labor cost vs. Total Compensation Revenue Percent, you can see the complete cost of human capital. Total Labor Cost Revenue Percent shows not only pay and benefits, but also the cost of contingent labor.

7. **Training Investment Factor** =
$$\frac{\text{Total training cost}}{\text{Headcount}}$$

8. **Cost per Hire**
$$\frac{\text{Advertising} + \text{Agency fees} + \text{Employee referrals} + \text{Travel cost of applicants \& staff} + \text{Relocation costs} + \text{Recruiter pay \& benefits}}{\text{Operating expenses}}$$

9. **Health Care Costs per Employee**
$$\frac{\text{Total cost of health care benefits}}{\text{Total employees}}$$

10. **Turnover Costs** =
$$\text{Cost to terminate} + \text{Cost per hire} + \text{Vacancy cost} + \text{Learning curve loss}$$

*Exclude payments for time not worked.

Sources: Saratoga Institute; William Brown, PhD., *HR Magazine*, January 2000

hrm5.pmd

1420 Monitor Road • San Diego • California • 92110-1545 • (619) 275-6528 • Fax (619) 275-0324

STEP 5:
CURRENT STATE PEOPLE ASSESSMENT: SWOT

Internal to the Organization

Strengths—"Build On"	Weaknesses—"Eliminate/Cope"

External to the Organization

Opportunities—"Exploit"	Threats—"Ease/Lower"

hrm5.pmd

1420 Monitor Road • San Diego • California • 92110-1545 • (619) 275-6528 • Fax (619) 275-0324

CORE VALUES IMPORTANCE = CORE COMPETENCE

Note: in the well researched book, *Built to Last*, and others, the creation of a strong core values system and culture led by the behaviors of the Senior Leadership is the only true competitive edge over the long term for any organization...and your #1 Core Competence.

Question: What are three simple ways Senior Leadership can reinforce and create this strong core values system in any organization?

Weekly
1. At each senior executive staff meeting, take 5 minutes and canvass the team for current examples of people who have used the core values as guidance to successfully achieve some positive results.
2. And then communicate this in a memo or email to all employees right away.

Quarterly
3. Set up a quarterly Olympic Style Recognition Program led by Senior Management throughout the organization to publicly celebrate those people who have been nominated by anyone for achieving positive results through following a few core values you want to reinforce (such as cost-savings, customer service, responsiveness, etc.)
4. Do the same kind of Leadership Recognition Program for management members only on a quarterly basis, using the Centre's Six Natural Core Leadership Competencies as a framework for selecting which few ones you want to emphasize that fit with your Core Values as well. Use your quarterly Strategic Change Steering Committee Meeting as the place to publicly celebrate these managers as well.

Yearly
5. Have everyone evaluated on their adherence to all core values as a part of their Performance Appraisal Process. Use the Centre's simple 4-page Evaluation to do this.
6. Conduct a simple 10-20 question yearly Employee Satisfaction Survey of all employees on how well all parts of the organization are adhering to each of the Core Values.

hrm5.pmd

CONTRIBUTION OF HR ACTIVITIES TO ORGANIZATIONAL EFFECTIVENESS

A Greater Contribution:

- Leading organizational change initiatives 58%
- Working with operating management 46%
- Business strategy development 46%
- HR strategy development 35%

A Lesser Contribution:

- Dealing with individual employee issues 15%
- Dealing with HR compliance/legal issues 14%
- Administering HR programs 13%
- Developing HR staff 10%

Source: the *1997 Survey of Human Resource Trends Report*, Exhibit 13, SHRM & Aon Consulting)

Contribution to Organizational Effectiveness

	Lower	Higher
Higher	• Dealing with HR compliance or legal issues • Dealing with individual employee issues	• Leading organization change initiatives • Working with operating managers
Lower	• Developing new HR programs • Selecting or managing vendors	• Business strategy development • HR strategy development

Time Spent on Activity

HR Professionals need to reassess how they allocate their time.

Source: the *1997 Survey of Human Resource Trends Report*, Exhibit 14, SHRM & Aon Consulting)

hrm5.pmd

1420 Monitor Road • San Diego • California • 92110-1545 • (619) 275-6528 • Fax (619) 275-0324

Building the dot.com HR Organization

HR can be more e-ffective

e-humanresources

e-benefits/compensation

e-recruitment

e-personnel

e-training

e-technology

Some suggested websites:

1. shrm.org — all of HR/association
2. hr.com—all of HR
3. hrvillage.com—all of HR
4. workindex.com—HR Best Practices
5. hrexecutive.com—magazine
6. workforce.com—magazine
7. ASTD.org—all of training
8. trainseek.com—training
9. instigo.com—management seminar
10. connect4training.com—training
11. trainingbroker.com—training
12. learn2.com—training
13. careerbuilder.com—career development
14. monster.com—recruiting
15. wetfeet.com—recruiting
16. jobs.com—recruiting
17. ework.com—recruiting
18. hrsmart.com—recruiting
19. dice.com—IT recruiting
20. hrplus.com—pre-employment background checks
21. lhh.com—Lee Hecht Harrison (outplacement)
22. nextjump.com—benefits
23. employeelife.com—benefits

hrm5.pmd

1420 Monitor Road • San Diego • California • 92110-1545 • (619) 275-6528 • Fax (619) 275-0324

CREATING "THE PEOPLE EDGE"
10 BEST HUMAN RESOURCE PRACTICES & 5 ABSOLUTES

Question: What of these 15 best HR practices do we use today in creating the people edge?

I. Structure
_____ 1. Create a **common HR systems framework** and terminology on Strategic HR Management.
_____ 2. Create a successful **Executive/Employee Development Board(s)** and processes.
_____ 3. Develop and implement an **HR Department Strategic Plan.**

II. Content
_____ 4. You win the game on **hiring/selection**—more than development alone.
_____ 5. With limited development funds, the key to organizational success is a **leadership development system**. Focusing first on the skills of trainer–coach–facilitator–influencer...and self-mastery.
_____ 6. Match up individual needs and organizational needs through tieing **succession planning and development** to career and Strategic Life Planning.

III. Process
_____ 7. Tap the **"discretionary effort"** of all employees. Use their hearts and minds in support of your business (not just their hands). Work towards **empowering** each of them as they are ready, willing and able.
_____ 8. Use your organization's core goals/strategies and core values as the "organizing framework" for your **performance management system** (including all job descriptions) to coach/sustain high performance.
_____ 9. Tie your **total rewards system** (pay and non-pay) to your organization's strategic plan—and create a "manager of rewards" position vs. the old "manager of compensation."
_____ 10. "People support what they help create"—People want involvement in all decisions that effect them prior to the decisions being made. Use **participative management techniques**.

IV. And the Five Absolutes
_____ 11. Treat all people with **dignity and respect** (the "Golden Rule") regardless of yours and their relative roles.
_____ 12. Feedback is *the breakfast of champions*—create **HR measurements** and "learn to speak finance, not English."
_____ 13. Make sure the **"KISS" Principle** is applied to all of these practices/policies.
_____ 14. **Rewards for teamwork** are clear and specific (functional, and especially cross-functional).
_____ 15. **Recognition programs** in place to recognize results at least quarterly (not suggestion programs).

Less Is More!

hrm5.pmd

1420 Monitor Road • San Diego • California • 92110-1545 • (619) 275-6528 • Fax (619) 275-0324

BECOMING A STRATEGIC PARTNER

Instructions: Please rate yourself on the following items. Use the following scale:

1. _____ Knowing my organization's business.
2. _____ Managing complexity.
3. _____ Anticipating pressures for organizational change.
4. _____ Responding appropriately to pressures for organizational change.
5. _____ Knowing line managers' goals.
6. _____ Reading Strategic Plans.
7. _____ Understanding Strategic Plans.
8. _____ Asking human resource questions.
9. _____ Simplifying complex ideas so that those not in the HR function can understand and use them.
10. _____ Thinking strategically.
11. _____ Being candid.
12. _____ Being a sounding board for others.
13. _____ Being available.
14. _____ Managing upward.
15. _____ Developing confidences.
16. _____ Working behind the scenes.
17. _____ Sharing the bad news.
18. _____ Confronting effectively when needed.
19. _____ Being loyal to the organization.
20. _____ Being perceived as capable by non-HR people.

_____ **Total (possible 200 points)**

hrm5.pmd

1420 Monitor Road • San Diego • California • 92110-1545 • (619) 275-6528 • Fax (619) 275-0324

SUPPORTING CREATIVITY AND INNOVATION
(BEST PRACTICES RESEARCH COMPILATION)

Instruction #1: Please answer each question on a 1-5 scale. Do you do this?

```
  1        2        3        4        5
  ├────────┼────────┼────────┼────────┤
 no     rarely somewhat usually   yes
```

I. **Ownership**

____ 1. *Love What You Do*–and help others find jobs to do what they really are passionate about. Help them find WIIFM (What's In It For Me).

____ 2. *Empower Others*–with clear expectations, guidelines and the support to succeed.

____ 3. *Keep a Light Touch*–know when to leave them alone and when to "shape" their environment and keep them *in-bounds.*

____ 4. *Promote Ownership*–self-initiative and a sense of responsibility.

____ **Sub Total for "Ownership"**

II. **Support**

____ 5. *Overcome Obstacles*–that prevent others from being creative and innovative.

____ 6. *Protect Them From Too Much Stress*–burn-out and rust-out are both wrong; the middle ground of energy and pressure is best for learning.

____ 7. *Use Brainstorming and Mind Mapping*–as well as other creative processes on a regular basis.

____ 8. *Provide Adequate Resources*–and the tools and training to succeed.

____ **Sub Total for "Support"**

III. **Communications**

____ 9. *Active Listening*–to give others a full hearing and the respect their ideas deserve.

____ 10. *Tolerate Ambiguity*–have few rules and policies, yet be deadly serious and consistent about them.

____ 11. *Provide Access to Voluminous Information*–of all types, including the business, the plans, the financials, and anything else they might want. The criteria of "need to know" is obsolete.

____ 12. *Be Responsive to New Ideas*–and look for the "nuggets" in them, versus why they won't work.

____ **Sub Total for "Communications"**

IV. **Feedback**

____ 13. *Reward Others*–for creativity, new ideas and follow-through, and continuous improvement, with a focus on positive recognition, new learning and growth opportunities as well as financially.

____ 14. *Debrief Projects and Events*–to create recognition and learning from experiences and for future creativity.

____ 15. *Balance Your Knowledge About a Topic*–there is a danger of knowing too much or of knowing too little. Abdication and micro-management are both wrong.

____ 16. *Strong Performance Expectations and Accountability*–are helpful if used to guide direction, clarity and channel energy. Goal setting is the #1 criteria for success in all the literature.

____ **Sub Total for "Feedback"**

hrm5.pmd

continued

1420 Monitor Road • San Diego • California • 92110-1545 • (619) 275-6528 • Fax (619) 275-0324

SUPPORTING CREATIVITY AND INNOVATION
(BEST PRACTICES RESEARCH COMPILATION)

V. Growth

_____ 17. *Allow Sensible Risk-Taking*–and small failures as learning experiences.

_____ 18. *Stress Continuous Improvement*–and reward progress, not perfection. Quality Improvement in your Daily Work (QIDW) is key.

_____ 19. *Provide Developmental Activities*–to keep their minds active and their hearts fertile.

_____ 20. *Develop a Shared Consensus on the "What" Only*–and leave the "how to" up to others' imagination.

_____ **Sub Total for "Growth"**

VI. Systems View

_____ 21. *Keep the Long Term in Mind*–and don't sweat the small stuff.

_____ 22. *Take a Broader Systems View*–in order to get the right perspective and multiple causes and goals for difficult problems and puzzles. Use cross-functional teams whenever possible.

_____ 23. *Keep the Big Picture in Mind at All Time*–and help others to have the ability to see it also. Use outside stakeholders to ensure the broader perspective (i.e., customers, suppliers, associations, partnerships).

_____ 24. *Provide a Team Environment*–and broader cooperation by actively promoting and modeling it yourself. Use cross-functional teams whenever possible.

_____ **Sub Total for "Systems View"**

Determing Average Scores					
_____	Ownership/4	=	Average	=	_____
_____	Support/4	=	Average	=	_____
_____	Communications/4	=	Average	=	_____
_____	Feedback/4	=	Average	=	_____
_____	Growth/4	=	Average	=	_____
_____	Systems View/4	=	Average	=	_____
_____	**Total/24**	=	Average	=	_____

Note: Maximum total score = 120 points
An average total score = 72 points
Instruction #2:

List your top 3-5 areas of excellence	List your top 3-5 areas needing most improvement
1.	1.
2.	2.
3.	3.
4.	4.
5.	5.

hrm5.pmd

1420 Monitor Road • San Diego • California • 92110-1545 • (619) 275-6528 • Fax (619) 275-0324

STEP 6:
SIX PEOPLE EDGE BEST PRACTICE AREAS

Best Practices Research: Over 30 authors research (see HR bibliography)

Centre for Strategic Management	Key HR Authors
1. Acquiring the Desired Workforce	1. 6 out of 8 had a similar item
2. Engaging the Workforce	2. 8 out of 8 had a similar item
3. Organizing High Performance Teams	3. 1 out of 8 had a similar item
4. Creating a Learning Organization	4. 5 out of 8 had a similar item
5. Facilitating Cultural Change	5. 5 out of 8 had a similar item
6. Collaborating With Stakeholders	6. 5 out of 8 had a similar item

Note: • None had all 6 competencies.
       • Only 2 out of 8 even had any of the beginning elements of a systems oriented approach to strategic human resource management and planning

CSM does not do basic research. We do **action research** as well as summarize and synthesize the research of others. We are **translators and interpreters**.

hrm5.pmd

1420 Monitor Road • San Diego • California • 92110-1545 • (619) 275-6528 • Fax (619) 275-0324

PEOPLE MANAGEMENT STRATEGIES

Instructions: Based on your assessment using our People Best Practices - Organizational Assessment, list below the key areas where your organization needs to place greater attention in creating attunement with its people management strategies.

Area 1   *Acquiring the Desired Workforce*

Area 2   *Engaging the Workforce*

Area 3   *Organizing High Performance Teams*

Area 4   *Building a Learning Organization*

Area 5   *Facilitating Cultural Change*

Area 6   *Collaboration With Stakeholders*

hrm5.pmd

"HOW TO" WORK WITH CEOs AND SENIOR EXECUTIVES

1. Focus on their needs, timing, priorities.
   - not mine
   - low ego
   - get results

2. Give options vs. "telling them" (ask questions).
   - valid information
   - informed choice
   - have alternative recommendations
   - internal commitment

3. Model openness, disclosure first — build intimacy.

4. Clear contracting — know what to expect.
   - "no surprises"
   - "good trooper" after decision

5. "Talk their talk"
   - ROI — business — industry — data — facts — limited resources

6. Truly care for them — personal relationship — build total confidence/confidences
   - acceptance
   - genuineness
   - empathy

7. Use "thank you" cards.
   - recognition
   - reinforce positives (not negatives)

8. Educate them by osmosis — mini lecturettes — models — vignettes (unfreeze them).

9. Share a systems model — fit — integration of parts.

10. Appreciate their web of relationships and complexities.
    - concise communications
    - bottom line/backwards thinking first

Tap into their dreams — visions — values
(Reinforce this)

hrm5.pmd

1420 Monitor Road • San Diego • California • 92110-1545 • (619) 275-6528 • Fax (619) 275-0324

Core People Strategies

#1 What is your Corporate Strategy regarding people (list it here)?

_____

_____

_____

#2 What are your Core People Strategies?
(3 - 7 max) that support the corporate People Strategies above

Strategies	#3 and Yearly Top Priority Actions
1.	**1.**
	1
	2
	3
2.	**2.**
	1
	2
	3
3.	**3.**
	1
	2
	3
4.	**4.**
	1
	2
	3
5.	**5.**
	1
	2
	3
6.	**6.**
	1
	2
	3
7.	**7.**
	1
	2
	3

hrm5.pmd

1420 Monitor Road • San Diego • California • 92110-1545 • (619) 275-6528 • Fax (619) 275-0324

THE CASCADE OF PLANNING™
The Systems Thinking Approach™

"STRATEGIC CONSISTENCY AND OPERATIONAL FLEXIBILITY"

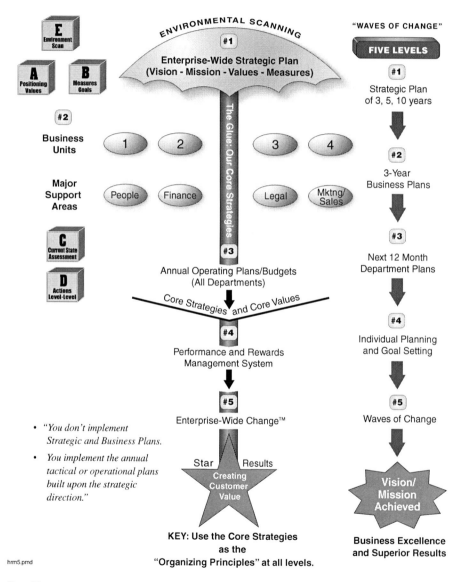

- *"You don't implement Strategic and Business Plans.*
- *You implement the annual tactical or operational plans built upon the strategic direction."*

KEY: Use the Core Strategies as the "Organizing Principles" at all levels.

Business Excellence and Superior Results

hrm5.pmd

1420 Monitor Road • San Diego • California • 92110-1545 • (619) 275-6528 • Fax (619) 275-0324

STEP 7:

Department: _____

Date: _____
Fiscal Year _____

ANNUAL "WORK PLAN" FORMAT
(AND FOR FUNCTIONAL/DIVISION WORK PLANS ALSO)

_____ : Strategy/Goals: _____

Yearly Pri #	Action Items (Actions/Objectives/How?)	Support/Resources Needed	Who Responsible?	Who Else to Involve?	When Done?	How to Measure? (Optional)	Status

hrm5.pmd

1420 Monitor Road • San Diego • California • 92110-1545 • (619) 275-6528 • Fax (619) 275-0324

PEOPLE BUDGETING

The "Business Case" Imperative

or

"Speak Finance, Not English"

BUSINESS CASE RATIONALE

"SPEAK FINANCE – NOT ENGLISH"

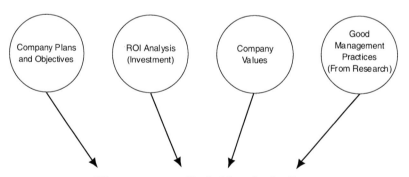

Company Plans and Objectives

ROI Analysis (Investment)

Company Values

Good Management Practices (From Research)

Why we recommend to do this project/staffing!

hrm5.pmd

1420 Monitor Road • San Diego • California • 92110-1545 • (619) 275-6528 • Fax (619) 275-0324

STEP 8: PLAN-TO-IMPLEMENT
CONTENT — PROCESS — STRUCTURE

THE ICEBERG THEORY AND SYSTEMIC CHANGE
(To Achieve Your Competitive Business Edge)

Efforts:

13%

87%

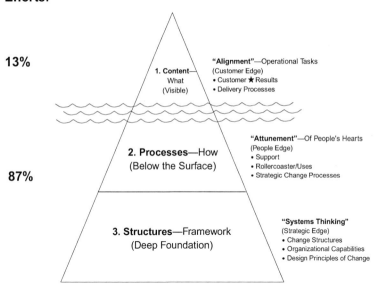

1. **Content**—
What
(Visible)

"Alignment"—Operational Tasks
(Customer Edge)
• Customer ★ Results
• Delivery Processes

2. **Processes**—How
(Below the Surface)

"Attunement"—Of People's Hearts
(People Edge)
• Support
• Rollercoaster/Uses
• Strategic Change Processes

3. **Structures**—Framework
(Deep Foundation)

"Systems Thinking"
(Strategic Edge)
• Change Structures
• Organizational Capabilities
• Design Principles of Change

Strategic Change requires a major focus on structures and processes
as well as content in order to achieve the content/results desired

---

Content Myopia
is
Our failure to focus on processes and structures
–yet–
Successful change is dependent on processes and structures

---

hrm5.pmd

1420 Monitor Road • San Diego • California • 92110-1545 • (619) 275-6528 • Fax (619) 275-0324

PRIMARY STRATEGIC CHANGE MANAGEMENT (STRUCTURES AND ROLES)

"A Menu"

1. **Visionary Leadership** — CEO/Senior Executives with **Personal Leadership Plans (PLPs)**
   - For repetitive stump speeches and reinforcement
   - To ensure fit/integration of all parts & people towards the same vision/values
*2. **Internal Support Cadre** (informal/kitchen cabinet)
   - For day-to-day coordination of implementation process
   - To ensure the change structures & processes don't lose out to day-to-day
3. **Executive Committee**
   - For weekly meetings and attention
   - To ensure follow-up on the top 15-25 priority yearly actions from the Strategic Plan
4. **Strategic Change Leadership Steering Committee** (formal)—replaces or is the Strategic Planning Team (Subcommittees of #4: the Leadership Steering Committee)
   - For bimonthly/quarterly follow-up meetings to track, adjust and refine everything (including the Vision)
   - To ensure follow-through via a yearly comprehensive map of implementation
*5. **Strategy Sponsorship Teams**
   - For each core strategy and/or major change effort
   - To ensure achievement of each one; including leadership of what needs to change
*6. **Employee Development Board** (Attunement of People's Hearts)
   - For succession — careers — development — core competencies (all levels) — performance management/appraisals
   - To ensure fit with our desired values/culture — and employees as a competitive edge
*7. **Technology Steering Committee/Group**
   - For computer — telecommunications — software fit and integration
   - To ensure "system-wide" fit/coordination around information management
*8. **Strategic Communications System (and Structures)**
   - For clear two way dialogue and understanding of the Plan/implementation
   - To ensure everyone is heading in the same direction with the same strategies/values
*9. **Measurement and Benchmarking Team**
   - For collecting and reporting of Key Success Factors, especially customers, employees, competitors
   - To ensure an outcome/customer-focus at all times
*10. **Accountability and Responsibility System**—all levels
   - For clear and focused 3-year business plans and annual department plans that are critiqued, shared and reviewed, as well as individual performance appraisals
   - To ensure a fit, coordination and commitment to the core strategies and annual top priorities
*11. **Whole System Participation Team** (can combine with #8)
   - For input and involvement of all key stakeholders before a decision affecting them is made. Includes Parallel Processes, Search Conferences, Annual Management Conferences, etc.
   - To ensure a critical mass in support of the vision and desired changes
*12. **Rewards and Recognition Programs** (can combine with #6)
   - For recognizing and paying people for strategic management accomplishments
   - To ensure reinforcement of the Accountability and Responsibilities System
*13. **Organization Redesign Team**
   - For studying and recommending what redesign of the organization is needed
   - To ensure synergy of the strategies, structures, processes, policies, values and culture
14. **Environmental Scanning System**
   - For collecting data from the environment (SKEPTIC)
   - To ensure advance awareness of coming changes to the environment

*Subcommittees of #4: the Leadership Steering Committee

hrm5.pmd

1420 Monitor Road • San Diego • California • 92110-1545 • (619) 275-6528 • Fax (619) 275-0324

ROLLERCOASTER OF CHANGE

"Persevere" — The Key to Strategic Change

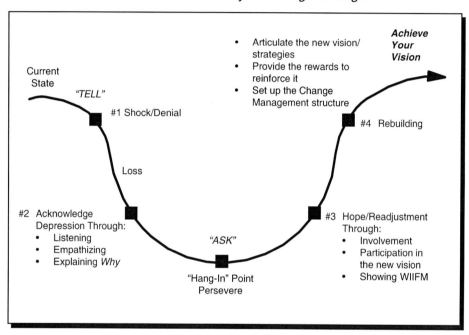

Major Questions

1. Not "if" but "when" will we start to go through shock/depression?
2. How deep is the trough?
3. How long will it take?
4. Will we get up the right (optional) side and rebuild?
5. At what level will we rebuild?
6. How many different rollercoasters will we experience in this change?
7. Are there other changes/rollercoasters occurring?
8. Will we "hang-in" and "persevere" at the midpoint (bottom)? How?
9. How will we deal with normal resistance?
10. How will we create a "critical mass" to support and achieve the change?

hrm5.pmd

1420 Monitor Road • San Diego • California • 92110-1545 • (619) 275-6528 • Fax (619) 275-0324

PEOPLE EDGE GAME PLAN FOR NEXT YEAR

1. Once a month, this plan will be reviewed at executive staff meeting.

2. Every three months we will have a big review and change management Employee Development Board meeting. Key focus will be our Core Strategies.

3. We have formed Strategy Sponsorship Teams on our Core People Strategies, using HR and line management personnel. At these quarterly meetings, each SST will report.

4. Every six months we will have a meeting with all HR and management/employees to review the status of our plan, along with future priorities.

5. After each monthly meeting, we will put out an Implementation Newsletter to the organization.

6. Each year we will conduct a Strategic Management Systems audit and review, and then update our strategic plan and our annual plans as a result.

7. Each year we will also conduct an environmental scanning process prior to our review and audit above.

8. Once our annual plans are developed, we will hold our Large group Review meeting again—to ensure clarity, agreement and commitment to it.

9. HR will be responsible to provide quarterly reports on results in "people management." Recommendations will be developed jointly with management each quarter on areas needing improvement.

10. Lastly, HR will partner with Line Management to ensure our planning for "people management" ensures our people become our competitive advantage.

hrm5.pmd

1420 Monitor Road • San Diego • California • 92110-1545 • (619) 275-6528 • Fax (619) 275-0324

STEP 9: "YEARLY CYCLE" OF THE STRATEGIC HR/PEOPLE MANAGEMENT SYSTEM

(TAKES TWO YEARS TO INSTITUTIONALIZE)

Date

June–**Year #1**	1.	Begin Strategic HR Planning (Plan-to-Plan: 1 day)
July-Oct	2.	Do Strategic HR Planning (5-8 days overall)
November	3.	Develop Annual Work Plans/Budgets
Jan–**Year #2**	4.	Conduct Large Group Dept. Plan Review (1 day)
Jan	5.	Conduct Plan-to-Implement (1 day)
April	6.	Quarterly Steering Committee Review Session – or bimonthly–
July	7.	Quarterly Steering Committee Review Session
September	8.	Evaluate Plan's Year #1 Success—Rewards based on this
Oct-Dec	9.	Conduct Annual Strategic HR Review (& Update: 2-4 days overall)
December	10.	Develop 3-Year Business Plans—HR Department
Jan–**Year #3**	11.	Develop Updated Annual Department Work Plans/Budgets
Jan	12.	Conduct Large Group Dept. Plan Review (1 day)
April	13.	Quarterly Steering Committee Review Session –or bimonthly–
July	14.	Quarterly Steering Committee Review Session
Oct-Dec	15.	Institutionalized—StrategicReview/Update Again— *as a way of life*

hrm5.pmd

1420 Monitor Road • San Diego • California • 92110-1545 • (619) 275-6528 • Fax (619) 275-0324

ANNUAL PEOPLE STRATEGIC REVIEW (AND UPDATE)

Annual People Leadership Review (and Update)

*"Similar to a yearly independent
financial audit and update"*

Goal #1: Assess the status of the Strategic People System and Executive/Employee Development Board.

Goal #2: Assess the status of any Personal Development Plan (PDP) achievement itself.

Resulting in:

1. Updating all Personal Development Plans.

2. Updating your Strategic Leadership Development System.

3. Clarifying your annual planning budgeting and Leadership Development priorities for next year.

4. Problem solving any issues raised in either goal.

5. Setting in place next year's Annual Plan, Leadership Development priorities and Strategic Change Management Process.

6. Refining your Leadership Development Board's process/focus.

hrm5.pmd

1420 Monitor Road • San Diego • California • 92110-1545 • (619) 275-6528 • Fax (619) 275-0324

PART C

A DEFINITION OF "LEADERSHIP"

Over the years, there have been dozens of versions of "the best definition of Leadership". We have all heard them—from the various leadership books being published, from the various workshops we have attended.

But the **best definition** of **"Leadership"**, by far, is the one that you subscribe to—the one that makes sense to you.

What are the important elements in a definition of **Leadership**?

How do you define **Leadership**?

LEADERSHIP IS:

Once you have completed your definition, please write it out on one of the flip chart sheets and post it on one of the walls. Then take a few minutes to check out some of the other definitions that have been posted.

Later today, at the end of this session, you will be given an opportunity to revisit your definition, to see if there are any amendments you would like to make, as a result of what you have learned through the day.

hrm6.pmd

1420 Monitor Road • San Diego • California • 92110-1545 • (619) 275-6528 • Fax (619) 275-0324

Qualities of a Good Leader

- they keep their temper.
- they explain things properly.
- they help you with things you don't know.
- they don't let people do whatever they want to do.
- they encourage you to do your best.
- they are fair.
- they love the people around them.
- they include everyone.
- their demands are reasonable.
- tell the people the truth.

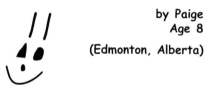

by Paige
Age 8

(Edmonton, Alberta)

Addendum
- and share their toys.

by Jillian
Age 3 1/2

(Victoria, B.C.)

hrm6.pmd

1420 Monitor Road • San Diego • California • 92110-1545 • (619) 275-6528 • Fax (619) 275-0324

LEADERSHIP

—U.S. Naval Academy

circa 1950s, updated 2005

- Know yourself
- Know your people
- Know your job

"Leadership is the most important thing we do here."

—Former Supt. USNA, Vice Admiral Lawrence

Passion

"What I think I bring to anything I do is passion. If I don't have passion, I don't do it. If you don't have passion in what you're about—go home."

—Jack Forness
San Diego Century 21 Co-Owner

Personal Senior Management Leadership

"Observing many companies in action, I am unable to point to a single instance in which stunning results were gotten without the active and personal leadership of the upper managers."

—Dr. J.M. Juran
Made in USA: A Break in the Clouds
Juran Institute, March 1990

hrm6.pmd

1420 Monitor Road • San Diego • California • 92110-1545 • (619) 275-6528 • Fax (619) 275-0324

IMPORTANCE OF PROFESSIONAL/SOUND MANAGEMENT AND LEADERSHIP PRACTICES

—THE ULTIMATE COMPETITIVE ADVANTAGE— (AND THE FOUNDATION FOR ALL ELSE)

The Leadership Factor

- Strong management without leadership becomes static and bureaucratic.

- Leadership without management is volatile and can become perverted by egomaniacs.

You Need Both!

GOALS OF THESE PRACTICES
Leaders do the right thing — Managers do things right

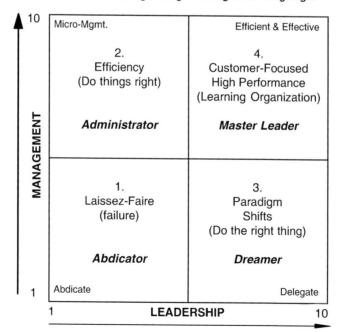

hrm6.pmd

1420 Monitor Road • San Diego • California • 92110-1545 • (619) 275-6528 • Fax (619) 275-0324

LEADERSHIP "AND" MANAGEMENT

	Leadership	"and"		Management
1.	Lead people/emotions		1.	Manage things
2.	Make change		2.	Improve execution
3.	Effectiveness		3.	Efficiencies
4.	Do the right thing		4.	Do things right
5.	Process/structure		5.	Content/task
6.	Setting direction/purpose/vision/ strategies		6.	Setting priorities/tactics to implement it
7.	Attunement with people's hearts and mind		7.	Alignment of the delivery system
8.	Meaning and passion/feelings		8.	Clarity and logic/thoughts
9.	Character/core values/cultural issues key		9.	Command and control
10.	Mobilize "adaptive" work		10.	Keep production/implementation going
11.	Creating/developing		11.	Sustaining/maintaining
12.	Leader-follower		12.	Manager-subordinate
13.	Coaching		13.	Directing
14.	Innovation/intuitive		14.	Administration/rational
15.	Personal responsibility and power		15.	Institutional role
16.	Curiosity/investigating/challenging		16.	Accepting
17.	What/why		17.	How/when
18.	Empower		18.	Delegate
19.	Long-term/future focus		19.	Short term/current focus
20.	Strategic/systems thinking		20.	Analytic/tactical thinking

hrm6.pmd

1420 Monitor Road • San Diego • California • 92110-1545 • (619) 275-6528 • Fax (619) 275-0324

LEADERSHIP AT ALL LEVELS

Servant Leadership

Leadership is one of the highest forms of service. It is best exercised when it freely motivates others to a decision that is really theirs—but which may never have been reached *without the leader's beneficial influence.*

—Unknown

- Executive Leadership
- Supervisory Leadership
- Operator Leadership

- Managerial Leadership
- Professional/Technical Leadership
- "Small Unit" Leadership (Cross-Functional Teams)

Commitment vs. Compliance

Leader — Follower — Commitment
Manager — Subordinate — Compliance

"To make a living is no longer enough.

Work also has to make a life."

—Peter Drucker, *Management*

Leadership Research Results

—Dale Carnegie Training Sponsors Research,
October 1996

A total of 658 employed adult Americans were interviewed by telephone in May 1996. "The results are extremely enlightening," says J. Oliver Crom, CEO of Dale Carnegie. "We find that, no matter what position an employee holds, **they view leadership the same.**"

Following is a brief description of the research results:

Leadership Defined
Three factors define leadership in the minds of American workers:
- Building relationships that establish personal **trust and credibility**.
- Regularly **communicating** in a **positive** way.
- Demonstrating **high integrity** in performing jobs.

hrm6.pmd

1420 Monitor Road • San Diego • California • 92110-1545 • (619) 275-6528 • Fax (619) 275-0324

LEADERSHIP DEVELOPMENT CONCEPTS AND DEFINITIONS

☐	1.	Tactical	and	Strategic
☐	2.	Management	and	Leadership
☐	3.	Range	and	Depth (of Leadership Skills)
☐	4.	Leadership Development	and	Executive Development
☐	5.	Training	and	Development
☐	6.	Teaching	and	Learning
☐	7.	Knowledge	and	Skills
☐	8.	Abilities	and	Attitude
☐	9.	Learning	and	Performance
☐	10.	Experience	and	Mastery
☐	11.	Program	and	System

What are the similarities and differences between these two sets of words as they relate to Leadership Development?

hrm6.pmd

1420 Monitor Road • San Diego • California • 92110-1545 • (619) 275-6528 • Fax (619) 275-0324

Best Practices Report
International Quality Study

American Quality Foundation (AQF)
and Ernst & Young

Summary of Study

- extensive statistical study
- 945 management practices over 580 organizations (84% response rate)
- in U.S., Japan, Canada, Germany
- automotive, banking, computer, health care industries

Best Practices Lead to High Performance (defined as:)

1. Market performance (perceived quality index)
2. Operations (productivity) performance (value-added per employee)
3. Financial performance (ROA)

Only Three Universally Beneficial Practices

- Only three (3) universally beneficial practices with a significant impact on performance regardless of starting position (rest is a "fit" question of organization – environment – performance)

   1. Strategic Planning/Deployment (Implementation)
   2. Business Process improvement methods (if focused on the customer)
   3. **Continuous broadening of your breadth and depth of leadership and management practices (to make additional gains in performance)**

Background

- Fundamental organizational activities — managing people, processes, technology, and strategy

---

What's the difference between the wise person and the fool?

They both make mistakes
but
the wise person continuously learns
from the mistakes and experiences of themselves
as well as others.

---

hrm6.pmd

1420 Monitor Road • San Diego • California • 92110-1545 • (619) 275-6528 • Fax (619) 275-0324

SEVEN LEVELS OF LIVING SYSTEMS

(TO BUILD SIX PEOPLE EDGE BEST PRACTICE AREAS)

Hierarchy:

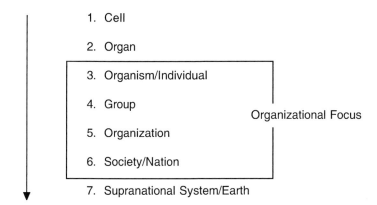

1. Cell

2. Organ

3. Organism/Individual

4. Group
                Organizational Focus

5. Organization

6. Society/Nation

7. Supranational System/Earth

Source: Kenneth Boulding

Our organizational focus is usually these four levels (#3,4,5,6) of the Living Systems—and the collisions of these systems with each other, both:

- within each hierarchal level (i.e., 1-to-1), and

- between each hierarchal level (i.e., group/department vs. organization)

> If you always do
> what you've always done,
> you'll always get
> what you've always gotten.

hrm6.pmd

1420 Monitor Road • San Diego • California • 92110-1545 • (619) 275-6528 • Fax (619) 275-0324

SIX RINGS OF FOCUS AND READINESS

(BASED ON THE SEVEN LEVELS OF LIVING SYSTEMS)

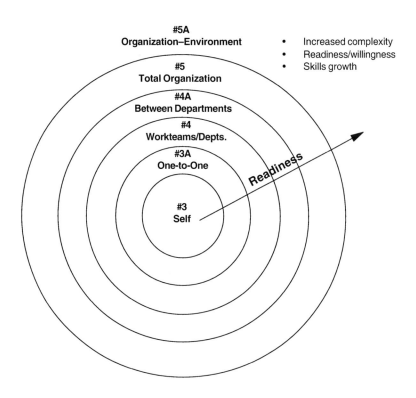

Note: Rings 3-4-5 are 3 of the "7 Levels of Living Systems"
Rings 3A-4A-5A are "Collisions of Systems" interacting with other systems

Source: Stephen G. Haines, 1980; updated 1988 and 2005

hrm6.pmd

1420 Monitor Road • San Diego • California • 92110-1545 • (619) 275-6528 • Fax (619) 275-0324

SIX NATURAL LEVELS OF LEADERSHIP DEVELOPMENT COMPETENCIES

BEST PRACTICES RESEARCH

Centering Your Leadership	27 Other Authors
1. **Enhancing Self-Mastery** (Level #1: Self)	1. 27 out of 27 had a similar item
2. **Building Interpersonal Relationships** (Level #2: One-to-One)	2. 17 out of 27 had a similar item
3. **Facilitating Empowered Teams** (Level #3: Teams)	3. 6 out of 27 had a similar item
4. **Collaborating Across Functions** (Level #4: Cross Functional Teams)	4. 3 out of 27 had a similar item
5. **Integrating Organizational Outcomes** (Level #5: Organization-wide)	5. 13 out of 27 had a similar item
6. **Creating Strategic Positioning** (Level #6: Orgn-Environment)	6. 9 out of 27 had a similar item

Note: None had all 6 competencies.

- Only 3 had four competencies
- Only 4 had three competencies

CSM does not do basic research. We do action research as well as summarize and synthesize the research of others.

We are translators and interpreters of Best Practices Research.

Leadership Development vs. Executive Development

Question: What's the difference between "Leadership" Development and "Executive" Development? Answer your Business Acumen.

---

hrm6.pmd

1420 Monitor Road • San Diego • California • 92110-1545 • (619) 275-6528 • Fax (619) 275-0324

ANAGEMENT®

MANAGEMENT SKILLS - BUSINESS ACUMEN

I. Executive Presence
Professionalism

II. Customer
Sales
Marketing
Merchandising
Advertising/Promotion
Service

III. Finances
Financial Analysis
Accounting
Budgeting
Treasury/Cash
Management
Capital Financing

IV. Technology
Computers
Telecommunications
Other Technology
Information Management

V. Products
Engineering
Design of Products
Product Knowledge
Manufacturing

VI. Delivery/Logistics
Purchasing
Distribution/Warehousing
Delivery Channels
Operations

VII. Administration
Legal Matters
Safety
Administration
Facilities

VIII. Human Resources
Recruiting/Selection
Compensation/Benefits
Employee/Union Relations
Development and
Succession

hrm6.pmd

EBHRM All rights reserved.

1420 Monitor Road • San Diego • California • 92110-1545 • (619) 275-6528 • Fax (619) 275-0324

SECTION VII
LEADERSHIP & MANAGEMENT DEVELOPMENT SYSTEM

"If we know one thing today ...
it is most managers (and leaders) are made, not born ....
There has to be systematic work on the supply,
the development, and the skills of tomorrow's (top) management ...
It cannot be left to chance...."
—Peter F. Drucker

Senior Management Defensiveness

This seems to be a very common situation in change programs, where managers reason defensively and "change" becomes just a fad. Change has to start at the top, as defensive senior managers are likely to disown any transformation in behavior or reasoning pattern coming from below.

—adapted from Chris Argyris
"The ForeSight Intrapreneur" #3, 1991

Management as a Profession

Managers generally don't devote the time and energy to skills that are essential for effective leadership management and communication.

What are they?
Why is it a profession?
How do you make this transition?
What should be the #1 Core Competency of every organization?

hrm7.pmd

1420 Monitor Road • San Diego • California • 92110-1545 • (619) 275-6528 • Fax (619) 275-0324

TAILORED TO YOUR NEEDS:
STRATEGIC LEADERSHIP DEVELOPMENT SYSTEM

Instructions: Please score this (H–M–L) on how important this is to do or have for your organization.

[A] **Step #1   Plan-to-Plan**

_____   • Have an Executive Briefing on Leadership (include reading CSM summary article on "Leadership" as preparation)

_____   • Form a Leadership Development Board and Support Team

_____   • Review *Best Practices Research*/Environmental Scan on Leadership/Development

_____   • Tailor the Strategic Leadership Development **System** to your needs

_____   • Make a commitment to proceed by Senior Management

Step #2   Shared Leadership Vision

_____   • Clarify the organizational Vision and Values

_____   • Tailor the CSM copyrighted **six leadership competencies and 30 skills** to your specific needs

_____   • Decide on executive level "Business Acumen" as well, and tailor its 30 knowledge and skill areas

[B] **Step #3   Leadership Success Factors**

_____   • Track and measure individual Executive Development progress

_____   • Track and measure overall Organizational Development progress

_____   • Provide the Executive Team with reinforcement

[C] **Step #4   Assessment of Leadership Competencies**

_____   • Self – Others (360°)

_____   • Competency Maps—for each management level

_____   • Other tailored assessments—leadership styles, etc.

_____   • What else?

Step #5   Leadership Development Strategies (& Actions)

_____   • Key organizational strategies for this Executive Development Plan/System

_____   • Administration and support structures

_____   • Rewards and Recognition tied to development

_____   • Succession Planning tied to development

hrm7.pmd

continued

1420 Monitor Road • San Diego • California • 92110-1545 • (619) 275-6528 • Fax (619) 275-0324

TAILORED TO YOUR NEEDS:
STRATEGIC LEADERSHIP DEVELOPMENT SYSTEM

Step #6   **Plan-to-Implement**
- • Establish Executive Development Plans for each individual at each level
- _____ – Senior Management
- _____ – Middle Management
- _____ – First Line Supervisors
- _____ • Have a Leadership Development Board meeting—"educate and organize" for implementation

D | **Step #7**   **Leadership Development Implementation**
- _____ • Apply coaching/mentoring skills
- _____ • Sharing/spreading our learning to our teams and others
- _____ • Organizational applications to improve Strategic Plan achievement
- _____ • Track, Report, Adjust the System
- _____ • Track, Report, Adjust each Executive Development Plan

Step #8   **Annual Leadership Review (& Update)**
- _____ • Yearly revisions/updates to the Individual Plans
- _____ • Yearly revisions/updates to the Leadership Development System

Parallel Process
- _____ • Create a culture for lifelong learning
- _____ • Stairway of Learning taught and understood
- _____ • Create both a supportive and challenging environment
- _____ • Stakeholder involvement

Who: _____

_____

_____

Create a Culture for Life-Long Learning	
Positive Culture • Stairway of Learning • Supportive, challenging environment • Positive reinforcement	**Key Stakeholders/Environmental Scan** • Customers • Suppliers • Board of Directors • Employees • Others

hrm7.pmd

"DEVELOPMENT" AS DEFINED AS . . .

Question: Which of these do we prefer?

Education	Job Assignments	Mentoring/Expanding
____ 1. public seminars	____ 13. current job adjustments	____ 26. mentoring others – shadowing – guide and confidante
____ 2. executive seminars — universities	____ 14. executive coaching	____ 27. being mentored
____ 3. Executive MBA	____ 15. committees	____ 28. professional associations
____ 4. customized, in-house training	____ 16. practicums — action learning	____ 29. community involvement
____ 5. guest speaker series	____ 17. job rotation	____ 30. intern programs
____ 6. conference attendance	____ 18. temporary job assignment	____ 31. supplier assignments/ relationships
____ 7. brown bag lunches	____ 19. job placement	____ 32. vendor, field, headquarters visits
____ 8. reading lists	____ 20. goal setting	____ 33. customer visits/ relationships
____ 9. self study	____ 21. "on-the-job training"	____ 34. buddy system — support each other
____ 10. train others	____ 22. job enrichment	____ 35. body – mind – spirit assessments
____ 11. outward bound team building	____ 23. task force	____ 36. job "shadowing"
____ 12. conference leader/ attendee	____ 24. "activity" assignments	____ 37. higher level meeting attendance
	____ 25. cross-functional task forces	

Leadership Challenge

The challenge for leadership is to build a corporate culture that builds self-esteem, sustains trust, preserves the dignity of work, develops human bonds, fosters open communications and allows dissent, and encourages growth and learning.

—Warren Bennis

And still makes a profit!

—Stephen . Haines

hrm7.pmd

1420 Monitor Road • San Diego • California • 92110-1545 • (619) 275-6528 • Fax (619) 275-0324

THREE LEVELS OF LEADERSHIP/MANAGEMENT DEVELOPMENT

(AND EXECUTIVES AS TRAINERS/COACHES)

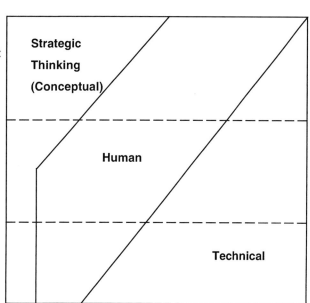

3. **Senior Management**
    ↓

2. **Middle Management**
    ↓

1. **Supervisors**

How do we develop our middle management and supervisors?

- •   Executives as trainers
- •   Professional trainers
- •   Development options
- •   Executive coaching and mentoring
- •   What else?

hrm7.pmd

1420 Monitor Road • San Diego • California • 92110-1545 • (619) 275-6528 • Fax (619) 275-0324

PERSONAL DEVELOPMENT PLAN: _____
Name

Development From: _____ to _____.

_____ / _____
Job Title   Date

Expected Outcomes (Knowledge/Skills)	Source/Method	H–M–L (Priority)	Date Complete	Authorized Signature
I. Enhancing Self-Mastery				
II. Building Interpersonal Relationships				
III. Facilitating Empowered Teams				
IV. Collaborating Across Functions				
V. Integrating Organizational Outcomes				
VI. Creating Strategic Positioning				

hrm7.pmd

_____
Supervisor Agreement/Date

1420 Monitor Road • San Diego • California • 92110-1545 • (619) 275-6528 • Fax (619) 275-0324

KEY LEADERSHIP DEVELOPMENT "STRATEGIES"

1. **Strategic Plan** as the correct context and tie-in for leadership development.

2. **Employee Development Board** (EDB)

3. A **Vision of Leadership** in your organization (values, beliefs, mindsets)

4. A set of **Six Natural Leadership Competencies** and skills tailored to your needs

5. A set of **Business Acumen Competencies** and skills tailored to your needs

6. **Succession Planning**/"Match" employee career development needs

7. On-the-job **development options** decided for your organization

8. Individual Development Plan for each management level **(IDP)** with 360 degree feedback (Executive, middle management, First line supervisors)

9. **Incentives, Rewards and Recognition** tied to IDP completion

10. **Reinforcement** (feedback/buddy system) set up

11. **Train trainer** of Senior Executives

12. Individual **Accountability Levels** (in Performance Management Appraisals)

13. **Roll down** from executives to middle managers and first line supervisors (3 levels of development)

14. Formalized **coaching and mentoring** set up

15. Annual Strategic **Review of leadership progress**

16. **Best Practices Benchmarks**

17. Use the entire Systems Approach to *Six People Edge Best Practice Areas* for your HR responsibilities as Senior Management.

18. **Core Skills and Values** - i.e. Self Mastery, Coaching/Counseling, learning how to learn/reflection time, training others, mentoring them, facilitating groups/teams and handling disagreements constructively

19. **A Leadership Development System** requires valuing the following behaviors: Integrity, Curiosity, Discovery and Dialogue

What else?

hrm7.pmd

1420 Monitor Road • San Diego • California • 92110-1545 • (619) 275-6528 • Fax (619) 275-0324

20 FAILURES IN LEADERSHIP AND MANAGEMENT DEVELOPMENT

(BEST PRACTICES)

Instructions: Which of these are you most likely to do or fall victim to (**H**-Highly Likely; **M**-Medium Probability; **L**-Low Likelihood.

_____ 1.   Not aligning with the organizational vision and core strategies.

_____ 2.   Not teaching and using Systems Thinking as a way to stimulate strategic and creative thinking and acting.

_____ 3.   Low ownership by top management and not modeling the skills and concepts presented.

_____ 4.   Low involvement by top management in attending training and development activities first; not helping teach management development as it cascades down to the first line supervisor.

_____ 5.   Not tied closely to a formal management/executive succession plan.

_____ 6.   No performance management system as a foundation, including a formal evaluation system used with all executives.

_____ 7.   Not using broad experiences and developmental methods.

_____ 8.   Focusing mostly on training courses.

_____ 9.   Focusing mostly on knowledge and awareness (vs. skills practice and attitude improvement).

_____ 10.   Not using adult (experiential) learning theory; mostly lecturing or films used.

_____ 11.   Not having a structured formal contract or Individual Development Process (IDP) as the framework for executives.

_____ 12.   Not holding managers accountable for development of others.

_____ 13.   Not having all training and development based on a tailored Competency Model tied to the Strategic Plan and future needs.

_____ 14.   Not integrating with and reinforced by other corporate/HR policies and practices.

_____ 15.   Lack of accomplishing development in intact departments/units and/or specific cross-functional teams for maximum reality and practicality.

_____ 16.   Not teaching core values and not holding people accountable specifically to them.

_____ 17.   Lacking personal and specific individual feedback (including a $360°$ feedback) as an important part of the development.

_____ 18.   Lacking an organized, comprehensive follow-up reinforcement system to integrate and build on the leadership/management development experience itself.

_____ 19.   Lacking action learning, research and presentations to top executives as part of the development so it is reality based and helps improve the organization.

_____ 20.   Lacking an Executive/Leadership Development Board to guide a formal set of goals or outcome measures and a tracking/evaluation process for the development system.

Total: _____H; _____M; _____L

hrm7.pmd

1420 Monitor Road • San Diego • California • 92110-1545 • (619) 275-6528 • Fax (619) 275-0324

YEAR #1: STRATEGIC CHANGE PROCESS

(TO ENSURE A SUCCESSFUL LEADERSHIP DEVELOPMENT SYSTEM)

Final Year #1 Task Check: As a minimum you need to . . .

_____ 1. Finalize your Strategic Plan and Leadership Development System.

_____ 2. Develop initial Personal Leadership Development Plans.

_____ 3. Hold supervisor review meetings of all PDPs and critique—then finalize.

_____ 4. Establish an organization-wide annual plan reflecting the strategic planning "action priorities" for the first year for each Core Strategy.

_____ 5. Align the budget to reflect the leadership/strategic planning annual priorities

_____ 6. Set up an ongoing quarterly Leadership Development Board to manage the change process (but start it monthly or bimonthly at first).

_____ 7. Establish a "Master Work Plan" for Year #1 implementation and follow-up. ("Yearly Map")

_____ 8. Establish a Leadership Key Success Factor monitoring, tracking, and reporting system/coordinator.

_____ 9. Revise the performance management and rewards systems (especially the appraisal) to support the desired leadership vision.

_____ 10. Obtain senior management's personal commitment to model and go first with this set of tasks as a monomaniac with a mission.

_____ 11. Identify Internal Staff Support Team and set up their development to ensure you build your own internal cadre of expertise and the **skills** (not just knowledge) to carry out your vision and core values.

_____ 12. Ensure key cross-department "Strategic Leadership Development/Change Projects" are set up with clear accountability.

_____ 13. Put in place a method through the Leadership Development System to also reduce costs, bureaucracy, waste & other obsolete tasks, including business process reengineering.

_____ 14. Identify list of why our change efforts might fail.

    • and determine what to do to prevent this from happening

_____ 15. Conduct an assessment of our collective leadership and where it is now vs. your Ideal Leadership Vision

_____ 16. Determine each department head's yearly operational "management system" to cascade this process further down into their entire organization.

_____ 17. Assess yourself vs. the _Six People Edge Best Practice Areas_ and 30 Specific Best Practices HR Programs and Processes.

hrm7.pmd

1420 Monitor Road • San Diego • California • 92110-1545 • (619) 275-6528 • Fax (619) 275-0324

"Blended Workforce" Gives Companies an Edge

Using a combination of employees—full time, part-time, temporary and outsourced workers as well as independent contractors—can save money, increase productivity, and improve customer service, according to Olsten Corp.

Of the employees responding to the study, 71 percent say their use of a blended workforce resulted in greater cost control, 64 percent report improved productivity, and 52 percent cite improvements in customer service.

Source: *HRMagazine*

"Blended" Workforce

A study conducted of 76 U.S.-based companies by William Olsten Center for Workforce Strategies yielded these best practices for implementing a blended workforce effectively.

- Establish clear boundaries and skill requirements for contract employees.
- Develop human resource policies and practices to support a blended workforce.
- Implement parallel selection criteria for core and assignment employees.
- Establish an integrated communications program.
- Use an on-site manager.
- Integrate contract workers into company teams.
- Provide job training to assignment and contract employees.
- Establish measurements for success.

Source: *Training & Development*

hrm8.pmd

1420 Monitor Road • San Diego • California • 92110-1545 • (619) 275-6528 • Fax (619) 275-0324

SECTION VIII
CREATING THE PEOPLE EDGE

SIX PEOPLE EDGE BEST PRACTICE AREAS

Best Practices Research: Over 30 authors research (see HR bibliography)

Centre for Strategic Management	Eight Key HR Authors
1. **Acquiring the Desired Work Force** (Level #1: Self)	1. 6 out of 8 had a similar item
2. **Engaging the Work Force** (Level #2: One-to-One)	2. 8 out of 8 had a similar item
3. **Organizing High Performance Teams** (Level #3: Teams)	3. 1 out of 8 had a similar item
4. **Creating a Learning Organization** (Level #4: Cross-Functional Teams)	4. 5 out of 8 had a similar item
5. **Facilitating Cultural Change** (Level #5: Organization-Wide)	5. 5 out of 8 had a similar item
6. **Collaborating With Stakeholders** (Level #6: Organization-Environment)	6. 5 out of 8 had a similar item

Note:
- None had all 6 competencies.
- Only 2 out of 8 even had any of the beginning elements of a systems oriented approach to strategic human resource management and planning

CSM does not do basic research. We do **action research** as well as summarize and synthesize the research of others. We are **translators and interpreters**.

hrm8.pmd

LEVEL I – ACQUIRING DESIRED WORKFORCE

Five People Edge Best Practices
1. Identifying organizational competencies.
2. Developing alternative workforce arrangements.
3. Conducting workforce/succession planning.
4. Installing a career development program.
5. Hiring desired employees.

Job — Person — Match

Executives spend more time on managing people and making people decisions than on anything else — and they should. No other decisions are so long lasting in their consequences or so difficult to make. And yet, by and large, executives make poor promotion and staffing decisions. By all accounts their batting average is no better than .333. At most, one-third are initially effective and one-third are outright failures.

— Peter Drucker
Harvard Business Review, July/August 1985

Stewardship and Value
A New Employment Covenant

The latest casualty of the changes sweeping through corporate America is the lifetime employment contract—the implicit agreement that provided employees with economic security in exchange for doing whatever work was necessary to keep the enterprise running. According to *Fortune* magazine, the new employment deal goes something like this:

"There will never be job security. You will be employed by us as long as you add value to the organization, and *you* are continuously responsible for finding ways to add value.

In return, you have the right to demand interesting and important work, the freedom and resources to perform it well, pay that reflects your contribution, and the experience and training needed to be employable here or elsewhere."

— "The New Deal; What Companies and Employees Owe One Another," *Fortune*

hrm8a.pmd

TOP TEN ITEMS OF THE
NEW EMPLOYMENT PACT

—Compiled by the Centre

1.   Employees need to seek "lifetime employability"—rather than job/employment security.

2.   The management of one's own career is accepted as a personal responsibility, not an organizational one.

3.   Continuous learning and skill development must occur to enable employees to keep abreast of the continuously changing work scenario.

4.   Executives and managers are beginning to appreciate employees as partners in the success of the organization.

5.   Managers set the overall direction and strategies for each work unit, based upon the corporate strategic plan. Employees are expected to set their own personal performance plans, in a synchronized way.

6.   Rewarding employees for results, not just for "doing their job" can produce a real "pay for performance system." Employee incentive programs can include long term success elements, such as stock options or bonuses linked directly to the organization's short term and long term business targets.

7.   Executives are expected to build a collaborative relationship with unions, as a partner in the overall success of the organization, rather than their more traditional adversarial stance.

8.   Strategic alliances and partnerships can provide numerous outsourcing opportunities.

9.   Employees can move between departments, between strategic partners on a lease-link system that matches existing needs with current, available resources in a timely and temporary arrangement.

10.   A variety of flexible work schedule arrangements—part-time, job-sharing, seasonal, contingent, and telecommuting—are the norm, with prorated benefit programs applicable to all of those people who choose one of these legitimate alternatives to full-time employment.

hrm8a.pmd

THE NEW EMPLOYMENT PACT
(Vs. OLD PACT)

The New Employment Pact

Responsibilities   **and**   **Rights**

What do I give (good or bad)?   What do I get (good or bad)?

The Old Employment Pact

What do I give?   What do I get?

hrm8a.pmd

1420 Monitor Road • San Diego • California • 92110-1545 • (619) 275-6528 • Fax (619) 275-0324

EXCELLENCE IN HIRING - A SYSTEM

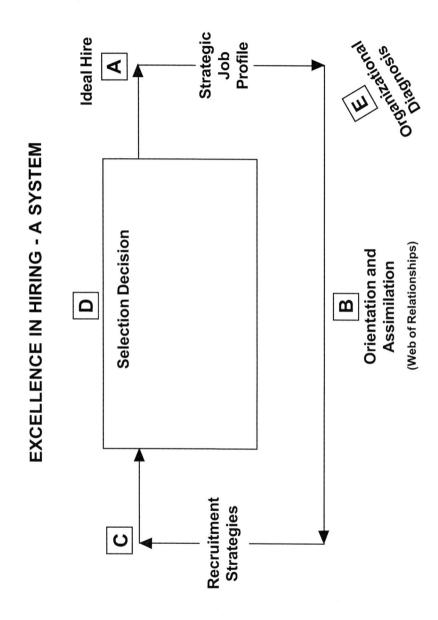

Ideal Hire

A

Strategic Job Profile

E
Organizational Diagnosis

D
Selection Decision

B
Orientation and Assimilation
(Web of Relationships)

C
Recruitment Strategies

hrm8a.pmd

1420 Monitor Road • San Diego • California • 92110-1545 • (619) 275-6528 • Fax (619) 275-0324

EXCELLENCE IN HIRING — A SYSTEM

A STRATEGIC JOB PROFILES (SJP) COMPONENTS

1. Job design
2. Roles (3-way)
3. Expectations/goals
4. Initial priorities
5. Challenges/problems
6. Resources available
7. Supervisor style
8. Qualifications, knowledge, experience
9. Personality/values
10. Management style
11. Mix of skills
   - technical
   - interpersonal
   - managerial/leadership
   - conceptual/strategic
12. Compensation/promote mediocrity
13. Employment contracts

D SELECTION DECISIONS

1. Decision meetings needed?
2. Fast vs. right?
3. Reference checks/secretaries/back doors — whose responsibility?
4. Resumes verified, especially education.
5. Dinner/informal interview (get to know the person).
6. Criteria is strategic job profile?
7. Biases of your own overcome?
8. Reasons why not to hire (if you "like them")?
9. Threatening/aggressive types (after hire) — come across as assertive.
10. Friendly types — can be "wimps" after hire.

"The potential to be equal to or better than . . . "

hrm8a.pmd

1420 Monitor Road • San Diego • California • 92110-1545 • (619) 275-6528 • Fax (619) 275-0324

D SUCCESSFUL HIRING

Do all hiring parties agree that successful hiring is most effectively done through:

Yes/No

_____ 1. Development of a Strategic Job Profile (SJP).

By when? _____

By who? _____

_____ 2. Use of behavior job interviews.

How? _____

_____ 3. Multiple interviews:

Who to do interviews? _____

_____

_____

_____

_____

_____ 4. A group decision process, comparing perspectives/open discussion, and based on the SJP.

When? _____

_____ 5. Checking full references and resumes.

Who responsible? _____

_____ 6. Checking past successes and working history.

Who responsible? _____

As a Guide to Future Success/Behavior

hrm8a.pmd

1420 Monitor Road • San Diego • California • 92110-1545 • (619) 275-6528 • Fax (619) 275-0324

BEST PRACTICES: RECRUITING AND RETENTION

"How to fill your staffing needs in the 21st Century"

I. SUCCESSFULLY FILLING SHORT-TERM HIRING NEEDS:

A. Finding Applicants:

1. Set up a Systems Thinking Approach℠ to Hiring

2. Create a Strategic Job Profile that everyone agrees to

3. Provide a significant Referral Fee for employee referrals-and publicize it widely—along with a yearly contest with big Grand Prizes for those employees who provided referrals

4. Use Online Recruiting such as Monster.Com

5. Go into good companies for the applicants you want that aren't job hunting right now

6. Set up Intern Programs for High School or College Students—Link with specific schools

7. Over hire for the current vacancies you have—create a talent pool of trainees

8. Recruit the entire labor pool, including minorities, different ethnic groups, etc.

9. Hold Quick-Hire Job Fairs where the applicants are hired on the spot

B. Selecting the Right Hires:

10. Go Fast-make it a top priority for all involved !!!!!!

11. Have the CEO (or a member of Sr. Management) involved in meeting the finalists if possible

12. Do something everyday to move the process along ("Swiss Cheese Approach")

13. Make sure the Hiring Manager is fully involved-it is not just the responsibility of the Recruiter alone (It is a Partnership)

14. Buy or merge with another, smaller company for its people

Guarantee Selection Success through a "Participative Decision-Making Meeting"

hrm8a.pmd

1420 Monitor Road • San Diego • California • 92110-1545 • (619) 275-6528 • Fax (619) 275-0324

BEST PRACTICES: RECRUITING AND RETENTION (Continued)

"How to fill your staffing needs in the 21st Century"

II. SUCCESSFULLY RETAINING LONG-TERM STAFF

1. Set up an Employee Development Board to manage this entire process

2. Create a Positive Work Environment/Culture that encourages people to do their best and ensure their personal fulfillment

3. Create a Balanced Work-Life for employees to have a life outside work

4. Create a way for employees to "contribute to society" and community in some way

5. Complete a yearly Succession Planning Process to identify "voids" and to promote "cross-functional movement/opportunities in the organization

6. Set up a visible Career Development and Ladder/Progression Process

7. Complete a yearly Workforce Planning Process to compensate for turnover, growth and promotions by identifying yearly needs well in advance of their actual openings

8. Set up flexible work hours, odd hour traffic routines, work at home, telecommuting, etc.

9. Set up job sharing and part-time work for alternative work pools such as students, seniors, retirees, the disabled, housewives, etc.

10. Identify pockets of high turnover and investigate them. Provide the managers with skills in coaching, conflict management, career development, etc.

11. Ensure that pay is competitive, even sometimes at the higher end of competitive

12. Set in place numerous recognition programs and incentive plans for specific functions.

13. Investigate non-traditional benefits and perks as a way to retain key employees

14. Consider outsourcing the work to individual sole proprietors and other companies

15. Train, provide tuition and Certify employees in return for obligated service time

hrm8a.pmd

ENVIRONMENT OF HIGH TURNOVER?

—Dr. John Sullivan

Asking people when they leave (why they are leaving?) isn't the same as asking them why they stay. Giving people more of what "they like" normally is just easier than fixing all of the "problems" or things they don't like.

There are several approaches to take. Ask workers why they stay using one of more of these tools:

1. Focus groups
2. Questionnaires, surveys
3. One-on-one with their manager (or HR)
4. Getting managers to talk to employees is such a powerful tool it beats the other options hands down.

Now I always split employee focus groups into **high performers** and then others later because I find it makes a bigger difference in productivity. I don't ignore the average employee, I just start with the ones that bring in the big bucks and have more choices to leave. CEOs like the split approach also.

As to what to ask them you probably already know them. Generally it's:

1. Why do you stay?
2. What do you like best about your job, co-workers, management?
3. What challenges/excites you?
4. What do you want more of and less of?
5. Describe your dream job.
6. If you ran the place, what would you do differently?

Training/coaching managers on how to do it is a bit of a problem depending on how good your managers are.

A second option is to educate your employees on what they can (should) expect from their managers. Although initially this will cause some waves, it helps force managers to return to the "basics" of good supervision. I usually suggest you tell them to expect:

1. Open two-way communication.
2. Recognition for good work.
3. An opportunity to be challenged.
4. An opportunity to grow and learn.
5. Some control over their work/work environment.
6. An opportunity to fix any negative aspects of their performance.

Question: **Is turnover a problem in your organization? If so, what do you need to do about it?**

hrm8a.pmd

1420 Monitor Road • San Diego • California • 92110-1545 • (619) 275-6528 • Fax (619) 275-0324

Workforce Flow FY '06 to FY '07
(Do For Each Year)

Company_____ Division_____ Date_____

Constant in Position		Tech	Supervisor	Manager	Director	Vice President	Sr. Vice President	Projected Turnover	Transfers
					Movement/Promotion →				
Start # Technical = 100		60	15					20	5
Supervisor = 50			30	10				5	5
Manager = 20				10	5			4	1
Director = 10					6	3		1	0
Vice President = 5						2	1	2	0
Senior Vice President = 2							1	1	0
(GAP) New Hires During FY		60	15	10	3	1	1	Turnover Sum: 33	Transfer Sum: 11
Desired Total Needed by end of FY '07		120	60	30	14	6	3		

hrm8a.pmd

1420 Monitor Road • San Diego • California • 92110-1545 • (619) 275-6528 • Fax (619) 275-0324

SUCCESSION PLANNING SIMPLIFIED

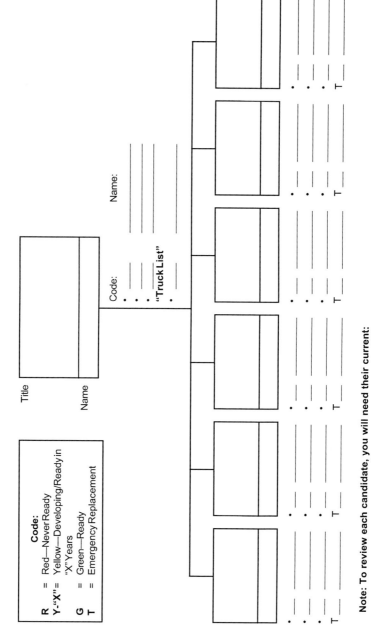

Code:

R = Red—Never Ready
Y-"X" = Yellow—Developing/Ready in "X" Years
G = Green—Ready
T = Emergency Replacement

Title

Name

Name:

Code:

"Truck List"

Note: To review each candidate, you will need their current:

1. Performance Appraisal Form
2. Career Development Form
3. Supervisor's Assessment and Potential Competency Form

hrm8a.pmd

1420 Monitor Road • San Diego • California • 92110-1545 • (619) 275-6528 • Fax (619) 275-0324

SUCCESSION AND DEVELOPMENT SYSTEM

Instructions: On the spaces provided to the left of the items, list your top 3-5 (A-B-C-D-E) priorities to get started building this system. Also list your lowest priorities (X-Y-Z).

_____ 1.   Organization-wide Strategic Planning in place

_____ 2.   Annual Plans and Budgets in place for all departments with clear accountability

_____ 3.   Executive/Employee Development Board established

_____ 4.   HR Strategic Plan developed, approved and committed to

_____ 5.   HR Department Yearly Plans and Objectives in place with clear accountability

_____ 6.   Desired Core Organizational Competencies defined to guide overall hiring

_____ 7.   Workforce Planning conducted to learn hiring/succession needs over next 1-2 years

_____ 8.   Clear and complete job profile and expectations for open jobs

_____ 9.   Interview – hiring – selection – promotion skills and decision making process vs. competencies – for Senior Management/other management

_____ 10. Giving and receiving feedback – plus – handling conflict skills for Senior Management/other management

_____ 11. Performance Management program, cycle and evaluation – Appraisal Form supports the Strategic Plan for each individual

_____11a. Mentoring and Coaching Skills course for Senior Management/ other managers to set clear goals and follow-up with each employee

_____11b. Performance Improvement Skills course for Senior Management/ other managers for day-to-day and periodic performance reviews

hrm8a.pmd

1420 Monitor Road • San Diego • California • 92110-1545 • (619) 275-6528 • Fax (619) 275-0324

SUCCESSION AND DEVELOPMENT SYSTEM

_____11c. Concurrent Performance Appraisal Skills courses for Senior Management/ other managers.

_____11d. Career Development Program and forms defined – for each individual's self-development.

_____ 12. Rewards and Recognition Systems – to reinforce high performance as well as the role of coaching/developing others by Senior Management/other management.

_____ 13. Succession planning/program and forms established – in a confidential way – for Senior Management's eyes only

_____14a. Individual Development Plans (IDPs) for each individual based on succession planning and career development.

_____14b. Alternate "Development" Solutions defined by senior management and available for IDPs of others.

_____14c. Needs analysis conducted and "Training" courses available for common needs.

Proactive Succession and Development

Change your organization from:

"**Openings** waiting for qualified people

to

Qualified people waiting for openings."

—*Steve Haines*

hrm8a.pmd

1420 Monitor Road • San Diego • California • 92110-1545 • (619) 275-6528 • Fax (619) 275-0324

SUCCESSION AND DEVELOPMENT PLANNING: "THE SYSTEMS THINKING APPROACH"

Questions to Answer to Tailor this Program to Your Needs:

1. What are your Purposes for this program (especially in regards to Development and/or Performance Evaluation and Promotions)?

2. What sets of data do you want? (Competency data, Performance data, Leadership only or Business Acumen data also, Career Development Form and Preferences, Resume, etc.).

3. Who is on the Executive Development Board that must lead this process? Are substitutes allowed?

4. How will you do the Succession and Development Process? Do you have the resources to carry it out.

5. Who will collect the Assessments and maintain the minutes? How will you preserve Confidentiality? Is everyone clear that "what is said here, stays here" unless otherwise specified?

6. What is the order or sequence that you will use over time to have your collective management included in this Succession and Development Process? Top down is preferred.

7. How many people do you need their Career Development Forms/Preferences? How are these people selected? How are they notified in advance?

8. Who will eventually see the results? (ED Board plus Supervisor, HR, Outside Coach?).

9. What will eventually be shared with the Candidates on the Succession List (if anything) as well as those who filled out their Career Development Form?

10. How (or should) you "roll-up" the data to get a full management/organizational Profile of your Succession Depth (i.e. strengths and weaknesses)? Who is accountable to lead this?

11. What actions do you need to take now to correct your lack of depth?

12. Will you have group Training Events for common Succession and Development needs as found in the Succession Roll-ups? Who is accountable to lead this?

13. Will each Succession Candidate be required to develop an "Individual Development Plan" as a result of their feedback? Who will approve it? Who will track its accomplishments and report it back to the EDB?

14. Will there be a follow-up Succession Planning session later on to ensure and assess the improvement of each Candidate? How far out do you want the Re-Assessment? Yearly?

15. How does this "tie-in" to the 360° Leadership Competency Development Assessment Program?

16. Will Executives and Managers receive Coaching and Mentoring Skills Training necessary to support this Succession and Development Program's effectiveness? Who is accountable to lead this effort?

17. What's your implementation Game Plan to phase it in over X number of years?

18. What else?

hrm8a.pmd

1420 Monitor Road • San Diego • California • 92110-1545 • (619) 275-6528 • Fax (619) 275-0324

360° LEADERSHIP DEVELOPMENT ASSESSMENT PROGRAM

Questions to answer to "Tailor the Program to Your Needs":

1. What are your Purposes for this program (especially in regards to Development and/or Performance Evaluation)? Is it voluntary? Who is the overall Internal Coordinator?

2. What sets of data do you want? (Competency data, Performance data, Leadership only or Business Acumen data also).

3. Who will collect the Assessments? How will you preserve Confidentiality? If people have questions, who can they call?

4. Will the scoring be On-Line (eventually), done by HR or by each Assessee?

5. What is the order or sequence that you will use over time to have your collective management take this Assessment? Top down is preferred.

6. How many "Other" Assessments will each of you send out? How are these people selected? How are they notified in advance?

7. Who will eventually see the results? (Self-Assessee plus Supervisor, HR, Outside Coach?).

8. What will eventually be shared with the "Others" who filled out the Assessment? Any thank you's to them afterwards?

9. How (or should) you "roll-up" the data to get a full management/organizational Profile of your Leadership strengths and weaknesses? Who is accountable to lead this? Do you want to use an "Organizational" version of this for all/parts of your organization instead?

10. Will you have group Training Events for common Leadership needs as found in the Assessment Roll-ups? Who is accountable to lead this?

11. Will each Assessee be required to developed an "Individual Development Plan" as a result of their feedback? Who will approve it? Who will track its accomplishments?

12. Will there be a follow-up 360° Competency Assessment follow-up later on to ensure and assess the improvement of each Assessee? How far out do you want the Re-Assessment?

13. How does this "tie-in" to Succession Planning and an Executive Development Board?

14. Will Executives and Managers receive Coaching and Mentoring Skills Training necessary to support this Assessment Program's effectiveness? Who is accountable to lead this effort?

15. What else?

hrm8a.pmd

1420 Monitor Road • San Diego • California • 92110-1545 • (619) 275-6528 • Fax (619) 275-0324

THE STANDARD EMPLOYEE "MISMATCH"

(OF THE HIGH GROWTH/ACQUISITION-ORIENTED ORGANIZATION)

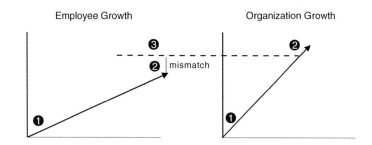

"When the organization's rate of growth/acquisition is greater than yours,
you will be left behind at some point."

—*Stephen G. Haines*

• Individual expectations become out-of-sync with organization needs over time.

HOW IT HAPPENS

I. Jobs go from broad and shallow to narrow and deep

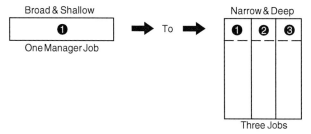

II. Once the 3 "narrow and deep" jobs are set up, a "new manager" of the three jobs is created with the same "title" but greater pay, expectations and competencies than old Job #1.

hrm8a.pmd

1420 Monitor Road • San Diego • California • 92110-1545 • (619) 275-6528 • Fax (619) 275-0324

LEVEL 2 – ENGAGING THE WORKFORCE

Five People Edge Best Practices
6. Installing a Performance Management System.
7. Linking compensation to performance.
9. Providing flexible benefits.
10. Dealing with poor performance.

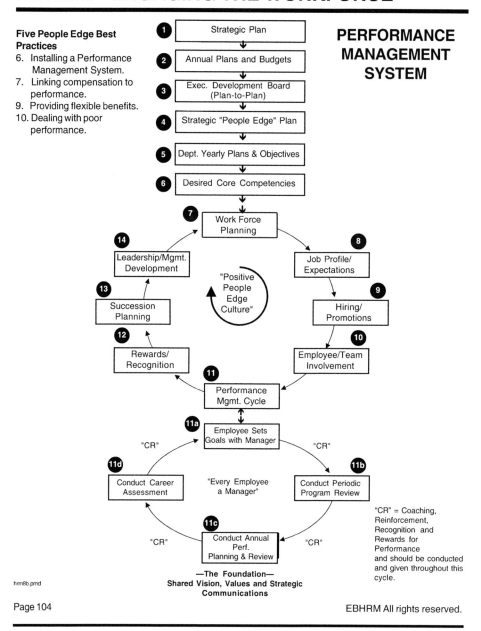

PERFORMANCE MANAGEMENT SYSTEM

1. Strategic Plan
2. Annual Plans and Budgets
3. Exec. Development Board (Plan-to-Plan)
4. Strategic "People Edge" Plan
5. Dept. Yearly Plans & Objectives
6. Desired Core Competencies
7. Work Force Planning
14. Leadership/Mgmt. Development
13. Succession Planning
12. Rewards/ Recognition
"Positive People Edge Culture"
8. Job Profile/ Expectations
9. Hiring/ Promotions
10. Employee/Team Involvement
11. Performance Mgmt. Cycle
11a. Employee Sets Goals with Manager
11d. Conduct Career Assessment
11b. Conduct Periodic Program Review
11c. Conduct Annual Perf. Planning & Review
"Every Employee a Manager"
"CR"

"CR" = Coaching, Reinforcement, Recognition and Rewards for Performance and should be conducted and given throughout this cycle.

—The Foundation—
Shared Vision, Values and Strategic Communications

hrm8b.pmd

1420 Monitor Road • San Diego • California • 92110-1545 • (619) 275-6528 • Fax (619) 275-0324

EFFECTIVE PERFORMANCE AND REWARDS SYSTEM

The Measurement of an Effective Performance and Rewards System:

No surprises:
- by the supervisor
- for the employee

at appraisal time and throughout the year.

HIGH PERFORMANCE EMPOWERING ORIENTED REWARD SYSTEM

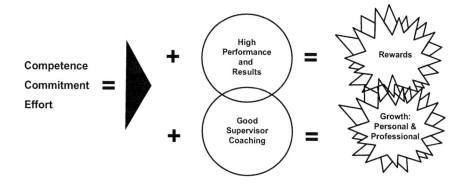

Competence

Commitment **=**

Effort

+ High Performance and Results **=** Rewards

+ Good Supervisor Coaching **=** Growth: Personal & Professional

hrm8b.pmd

1420 Monitor Road • San Diego • California • 92110-1545 • (619) 275-6528 • Fax (619) 275-0324

PERFORMANCE MANAGEMENT SYSTEM

The **Performance Management System** is a way of life in an organization when:

Which do you have?

Yes/No

_____ 1. Senior management provides the leadership, commitment, and ownership along with the appropriate modeling to the rest.

_____ 2. The Performance Management System's four main components — goal setting, progress views, yearly appraisals, and career development are effectively executed within the context of the Corporate Mission and yearly goals.

_____ 3. A Performance Management Audit Program is in place and operating successfully to ensure the Performance Management System is operating properly.

_____ 4. The Corporation successfully meets its goals, is very profitable, and has a one team concept and style.

_____ 5. The entire Corporation understands and properly perceives the Performance Management concept, system, and definition of "rewards".

6. Total rewards, both financial and non-financial, are applied appropriately based on the performance achieved both in terms of:

_____ a. job results at three levels of the organization (individual, team, and corporate); as well as

_____ b. Corporate behavior and values in the Corporate Philosophy, Management Principles, and Customer Service Creed.

hrm8b.pmd

1420 Monitor Road • San Diego • California • 92110-1545 • (619) 275-6528 • Fax (619) 275-0324

PERFORMANCE MANAGEMENT SYSTEM

Yes/No

_____ 7. All management personnel demonstrate the skills necessary to actively manage their employees according to these performance management practices.

_____ 8. Employees are aware of and meet their targeted and measurable goals and are satisfied with their performance and rewards. They are also motivated to achieve future results.

_____ 9. All poor performers have their performance confronted and corrected, or else removed from the jobs they perform poorly.

_____ 10. Employees and management have joint responsibilities for individual careers.

_____ 11. Our organization is known both internally and externally as a performance-oriented one that attracts, motivates, and retains people with this orientation.

Source: Imperial Corporation of America and Stephen G. Haines, 1986

Question: What actions should we take as a result of this analysis?

A Rewards System Should Be Strategic

In an unhealthy organization
the strategy lays out one agenda,
but the culture reinforces another.

In healthy organizations,
the Rewards System reinforces the
desired culture and vision.

hrm8b.pmd

1420 Monitor Road • San Diego • California • 92110-1545 • (619) 275-6528 • Fax (619) 275-0324

AN OLYMPIC RECOGNITION PROGRAM THAT WORKS

(REWARD AT 3 LEVELS — BRONZE — SILVER — GOLD)

Some Key Concepts

1. Select 1-2 key outcomes you want, based on your Strategic Plan, such as lower costs, improved customer service, etc. Reward results and achievement, not ideas or suggestions.

2. The key program nomination characteristics include:
   - Anyone can nominate anyone else or any team, including themselves.
   - Nominations are for anyone or any team who has actually achieved an outcome desired above.

3. Ideas and proposals are **not** rewarded; achieving actual results are rewarded (i.e. save $11.00, receiving a customer service thank you, etc.)

4. Publicize this program widely. Set up a simple one-page form on colored paper to fill out. Make the form widely distributed and available.

5. Hold large group meetings on a regular basis (quarterly?) with everyone eligible in attendance. If the organization is spread out, hold regional meetings and possibly one big annual meeting. It is best to make this meeting a quarterly business meeting with the *recognition* of winners as the main attraction. Some other business topics might include:
   - Discussion of Key Success Factors or outcome business results.
   - A guest speaker on a key topic, such as one of your key strategies or core values.
   - Discussion of 1-2 key core strategies and their importance and priorities.
   - Celebration of successes—social time such as a buffet lunch, end of day non-alcoholic happy hour, etc.

6. Set up a Peer Review Committee to review the submissions for documented outcomes. The goal is to get as many "winners" as possible; not to create winners and losers (multiple winners-compete against yourself only). Keep the results hidden until the meeting itself.

7. The basic concept here is **the "Olympic Games"**; bronze, silver and gold winners. Bronze is anyone who wins on any quarter meeting. Silver is all the big winners. And Gold is reserved for the top 3-5 biggest winners. Do not single out one big final winner!

hrm8b.pmd

1420 Monitor Road • San Diego • California • 92110-1545 • (619) 275-6528 • Fax (619) 275-0324

PERFORMANCE APPRAISALS . . .

TIED TO STRATEGIC PLANNING

Performance Appraisals
must be tied to support
#1
Your organization's Core Strategies (i.e., results)
and
#2
Your organization's Core Values (i.e., behaviors)
and
#3
Your own learning and growth (i.e., career development)

(If you are serious about your Strategic Plan)

— Result: A Four Page Performance Management/Appraisal Form —

❶

Cover Sheet
Summary
Evaluation

❷

Results	
Strategies	Plan/Actual
1.	
2.	
3.	
4.	
5.	

❸

Values	
Values	Plan/Actual
1.	
2.	
3.	
4.	

❹

Career Development
Objectives Action
1. __X__ : Plan ____
2 __Y__ : ____
3. __Z__ : ____

hrm8b.pmd

1420 Monitor Road • San Diego • California • 92110-1545 • (619) 275-6528 • Fax (619) 275-0324

CENTRE for STRATEGIC MANAGEMENT®

ROLES: INDIVIDUAL LEVEL OF PERFORMANCE

People Management Roles	Purposes	Documents
1. **Senior management**	a. To Clarify and carry out your individual leadership role	a. **Personal Leadership Plan (PLP)**
	b. To have 360⁰ feedback as a member of senior managment - as a leader - with business acumen too	b. **Individual Development Plans (IDP)** - 360⁰ Leadership Development Feedback - 360⁰ Business Acumen Feedback
2. **All management**	a. To have a clear Performance, Responsibility and Accountability Management System (PRAMS)	a. **PRAMS Program** installed
	b. To have 360⁰ feedback as a member of managment - as a leader - with business acumen too	b. **Individual Development Plans (IDP)** - 360⁰ Leadership Development Feedback - 360⁰ Business Acumen Feedback
	c. Performance tied into Strategic Plan	c. Simplified four page **Performance Appraisal**
3. **Entire workforce**	a. To have a clear performance, responsibility and accountability management system (PRAMS)	a. **PRAMS Program** installed
	b. Performance tied into Strategic Plan	b. Simplified four page **Performance Appraisal**

hrm8b.pmd

1420 Monitor Road • San Diego • California • 92110-1545 • (619) 275-6528 • Fax (619) 275-0324

PAY FOR PERFORMANCE DOESN'T WORK — BEST PRACTICES RESEARCH

Pay for Position and Reward for Performance

"Pay" Program Areas That Rarely Work Include:
1. Merit Programs
2. Bonus Programs
3. Job Descriptions
4. Hay System for Job Evaluation
5. Adjustments vs. Pay Range Changes
6. Promotional Increases
7. Stock Options

What Executives Want in a Pay System

1. **Variable vs. Fixed Compensation/Salaries**
   - Based on ability to pay (= profit)
   - Shared risk and reward
   - Lower long-term salary/benefits cost

2. **Tied Benefits to Performance vs. Longevity Only**
   - Cafeteria benefits
   - 401K investments
   - Profit/gainsharing vs. pension guarantee
   - Improved ROI (vs. 39-40% of pay today)

3. **Link "Pay to Performance"**
   - In a more comprehensive way
   - Rewards vs. pay
   - Total performance vs. individual performance

4. **Tailor Rewards to Different Jobs/Personnel**
   - That they can influence
   - Many different incentive programs/multiple goals
   - Cafeteria rewards approach to non-financial rewards

hrm8b.pmd

1420 Monitor Road • San Diego • California • 92110-1545 • (619) 275-6528 • Fax (619) 275-0324

BEYOND BASIC BENEFITS

— Nancy Hatch Woodward

Human resource managers are increasingly searching for new incentives to entice top employees to remain with their companies. "Retention is an important issue; not one you can turn on or off. You have to pay attention to it for the long haul, consistently day in and day out," says Dave Pylipow, director of employee relations at Hallmark Cards Inc. in Kansas City, MO., which has 12,000 U.S. employees—and a turnover rate of just over 6 percent.

Retention is determined by the way managers treat employees on a day-to-day basis, he says.

Innovative Benefits
Most HR managers agree that the first step in employee retention is to make sure the benefits package is competitive.

"Clearly, if you want to keep people, you have to make sure all your benefits and compensation programs are competitive and innovative," says Robert Hecker, vice president of human resources for UNUM America, a disability insurance firm headquartered in Portland, Maine.

First Tennessee, in addition to its profit-sharing program, has concentrated on benefits to help employees with work/life balance.

"In the early 90's, we started asking our employees what it would take for them to build loyalty and improve their productivity. They told us loudly and clearly that they wanted more flexibility and control of their work. We listened and developed an overall strategy of promoting commitment to work and family.

Source: *HRMagazine*

hrm8b.pmd

1420 Monitor Road • San Diego • California • 92110-1545 • (619) 275-6528 • Fax (619) 275-0324

EMPLOYEE BENEFITS AS A COMPETITIVE BUSINESS ADVANTAGE

— Fast Company

(AND A POSITIVE ROI IN THE YEARLY BUDGET AS WELL)

SAS Institute, Inc. is a software development company based in Carey, North Carolina with 1997 revenues of $750 million, double that of five years ago and employs over 5400 people. They have good cash flow and a very, very healthy balance sheet and profitability.

One of the key ways they have achieved this is through the use of the benefit programs as a competitive business advantage. Employees have everything they need and so they can totally focus on their work while at work.

These more costly and extensive benefit programs listed below are above and beyond those found at traditional companies. They are completely paid for by reduced turnover (and hence recruiting, hiring, relocation, unfilled jobs and start-up learning costs). SAS has ONLY 3.7% turnover a year in a high turnover industry and in a competitive Research Triangle location (and extra $12,500 per employee per year is available for benefits due to lower turnover).

The idea is to hire adults and treat them like adults, then they are expected to and will behave like adults. Here, what you accomplish is more important than how you appear. When you treat people well and are loyal to them, as SAS does, you get their loyalty. Once you've got their loyalty, they'll do anything for you.

This is a company built on accountability and documentation. SAS is managed lightly, but not casually. Every product manual includes the names of the developers and testers who created or updated the software!

A group at the company meets monthly to discuss proposed new benefits, evaluating them in the context of a three-part test.

1. Would it serve a significant number of employees?

2. Would the benefit be in accord with SAS's culture?

3. And, would it be cost accountable—that is, would its perceived value be at least as high as its cost?

hrm8b.pmd

1420 Monitor Road • San Diego • California • 92110-1545 • (619) 275-6528 • Fax (619) 275-0324

EMPLOYEE BENEFITS AS A COMPETITIVE BUSINESS ADVANTAGE

These unusual benefits from just *one* company include:

1. 35 hour full-time work week

2. live piano music in the cafeteria

3. unlimited soda, coffee, tea and juice

4. one extra week of paid vacation between Christmas and New Years

5. a 36,000 square-foot on-site gym that includes pool tables, ping pong tables, two full-length basketball courts, space for aerobics classes, weights, cardio machines, a dance studio and a skylit yoga room

6. two on-site day-care facilities, and one off-site facility

7. an on-site health clinic staffed with six nurse practitioners and two physicians

8. zero cost to employees for health insurance

9. dirty workout clothes laundered overnight at no charge

10. casual dress every day (except in client-contact situations)

11. elder-care advice and referrals

12. on-site massages several times a week

13. all family benefits extended to domestic partners, regardless of sexual orientation

14. unlimited sick days, and use of sick days to care for sick family members

15. advice and referrals on financial planning for college and retirement

16. your lunch tab is automatically deducted from your paycheck

17. and also all the usual traditional benefits other companies have

hrm8b.pmd

1420 Monitor Road • San Diego • California • 92110-1545 • (619) 275-6528 • Fax (619) 275-0324

BUILDING INTERPERSONAL COMPETENCE

Building Excellence

"Build on what a man (person) is—don't tear him down."

—Gen. Creighton Abrams

Managers' Morale Mistakes

In a personnel survey, 150 executives from the nation's 1,000 largest companies identified the ways in which managers damage employees' morale the most.

Criticizing in front of others	38%
Being dishonest	38%
Taking credit for others' work	12%
Being inaccessible	6%
Showing favoritism	4%
Don't know	2%

Source: Accountemps

Personnel Journal

Positive vs. Negative Reinforcement

The national average of parent-to-child criticisms is **12 to 1 — that is, 12 criticisms to 1 compliment.** Within the average secondary school classroom, the ratio of criticism to compliments is 18 to 1 between teacher and student. And we wonder why our children so often have low self-esteem?

—*The Magic of Conflict*

hrm8b.pmd

1420 Monitor Road • San Diego • California • 92110-1545 • (619) 275-6528 • Fax (619) 275-0324

CYCLES OF TRUST AND MISTRUST

INTERPERSONAL RELATIONSHIPS—ONE-TO-ONE

Cycle of Trust

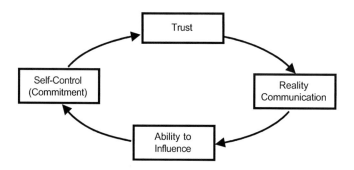

Cycle of Mistrust

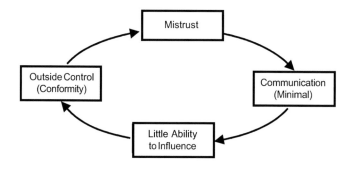

Source: Dr. Dale Zand, Professor of Business Administration, New York University

hrm8b.pmd

1420 Monitor Road • San Diego • California • 92110-1545 • (619) 275-6528 • Fax (619) 275-0324

The Ten Commandments of Powerful Listening

—Adapted from Dr. Tony Alessandra

Note: **The more senior position you occupy, the less you tend to listen—** *agree or disagree?*

1. **Fight Off Distractions**—Train yourself to listen carefully to others's words despite external distractions.

2. **Do Not Trust Your Memory**—Take notes. However, keep your notes brief, as listening ability is impaired while you are writing.

3. **Let Others Tell Their Own Stories First**—Then, you can tailor your discussion to their particular needs, goals and objectives.

4. **Use Feedback**—Constantly try to check your understanding of what you hear.

5. **Listen Selectively**—You must listen in such a way that you can separate the wheat from the chaff.

6. **Relax**—When others are speaking to you, try to put him/her at ease by creating a relaxed and accepting environment.

7. **Listen Attentively**—Face them straight on with uncrossed arms and legs, and lean slightly forward. Establish good eye contact. Use affirmative head nods and appropriate facial expressions when called for, but do not overdo it.

8. **Create a Positive Listening Environment**—Take great efforts to make sure that the environment is conducive to effective listening.

9. **Ask Questions**—Ask open-ended questions to allow them to express their feelings and thoughts.

10. **Be motivated to listen**—Without the proper attitude, all the foregoing suggestions for effective listening are for naught. Try to keep in mind that there is no such things as a disinteresting speaker; there are only disinterested listeners.

If you are really willing to learn how to listen, it will take a lot of hard work to learn the skills, and constant practice to keep them in shape.

hrm8b.pmd

1420 Monitor Road • San Diego • California • 92110-1545 • (619) 275-6528 • Fax (619) 275-0324

THE TWO GOALS OF "COACHING FOR RESULTS"

#1 Achieve the performance improvement results desired by the coaching.

#2 Maintain or improve the relationship between the two parties.

Which is more important?

True Change – Self-Esteem

True change is internally motivated.

The higher an employee's self-worth, the more likely he or she will want to change and develop to full potential.

Praise opens the door to self-esteem and thus to growth.

—Kate Ludeman, *The Worth Ethic*

---

hrm8b.pmd

1420 Monitor Road • San Diego • California • 92110-1545 • (619) 275-6528 • Fax (619) 275-0324

'How Am I Doing, Boss? Boss?'

Coaches, you're not coaching. A study of 1,149 people at 79 companies found that **satisfaction with managers' feedback and coaching was middling at best.**

Other findings: **"Performance management" usually consists of nothing more than a performance appraisal that happens only once a year, with little or no feedback in between;** there is little opportunity for employee involvement in performance reviews; performance isn't rewarded sufficiently; appraisals are late and focus on the petty and negative; managers don't follow up with employees *after* apprising them; and, ironically, even with all those shortcomings, performance management is perceived as taking a lot of time.

All of this is according to the national study, "Performance Management: What's Hot, What's Not," released earlier this year by Development Dimensions International, a Pittsburgh-based training and consulting company.

Overall satisfaction with coaching and feedback scored a lackluster 3.25 on a scale of 1 to 5, with 5 the best. Performance appraisal's effectiveness at helping workers do a better job scored 2.95 and satisfaction with appraisal-related management training 2.8. Training aimed at helping employees make better use of their own appraisals scored an abysmal 2.04—mostly because very few companies offer any such training.

The final irony: 57 percent of respondents were managers. "The findings confirm what we're hearing," says Linda Miller, a DDI manager who helped conduct the study.

Everyone knows they should do feedback and coaching, but it's still not happening.

—Training

hrm8b.pmd

1420 Monitor Road • San Diego • California • 92110-1545 • (619) 275-6528 • Fax (619) 275-0324

EXECUTIVE COACHING NEEDS

"Even the best athletes have coaches

and

even the top coaches have coaches."

(i.e., mastery level coaches)

Who is yours?

AS PART OF THE CENTRE'S SUPPORT

A part of each project the Centre for Strategic Management undertakes includes Senior Management one-on-one coaching and support.

This occurs a number of ways:

#1. On each visit we make, it should include at least one hour (minimum) of one-on-one coaching support time with the Senior Executive.

#2. Thirty minute telephone coaching conversations by the Senior Executive and the Centre in between each visit.

#3. Each member of the top management team who wants to excel and be as effective a human being and executive as they can be is also assigned a separate "coach" for 3-4 30 minute telephone coaching sessions per month.

These are crucial and are included in each project we undertake to ensure ownership, commitment, and transference of all work to the client organzation.

hrm8b.pmd

1420 Monitor Road • San Diego • California • 92110-1545 • (619) 275-6528 • Fax (619) 275-0324

EXECUTIVE COACHING AGREEMENT

Coaching Goals

1. Improve your leadership skills.

2. Enhance the achievement of the project or process you are now undergoing.

3. Improve yourself as an executive and human being.

How

You and the Centre Partner meet on a regular basis (i.e., monthly/bimonthly) as agreed upon to discuss achievement of the above goals (i.e., 2-4 hour, face-to-face meeting, plus 3-4 30 minute telephone coaching/discussions each month).

Roles

1. You both share and compare your perceptions of the status of the above goals in relationship to your leadership skills and current state.

2. We will play "devil's advocate" with you openly sharing feedback and perceptions of the organization, as well as our own.

3. Your role is one of curiosity: i.e.,
    *   self-observer
    *   learner
    *   detective, and
    *   investigator of your leadership

4. You are free to accept or reject any feedback received — incorporating only those items/perceptions you feel are accurate.

Actions

At the end of each session you will need to develop a "To Do" list for follow-up. It can include items such as "Think about...", "Consider...", as well as any specific behaviors, actions to undertake.

hrm8b.pmd

LEVEL 3 – ORGANIZING HIGH PERFORMANCE TEAMS

Five People Edge Best Practices
11. Developing team skills.
12. Developing small unit leaders.
13. Developing empowered teams.
14. Establishing participative management.
15. Developing team rewards.

STAGES OF GROUP DEVELOPMENT

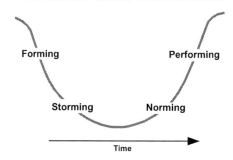

Four Stages of Teambuilding

—adapted from Will Schutz Associates

1.	**Forming**	1.	**Inclusion** • First stage of teambuilding • Do things with, share	• **Feeling:** Significance • **Fear:** Being ignored
2.	**Storming**	2.	**Control** • Second stage of teambuilding • Level of influence exerted • Degree that one takes charge	• **Feeling:** Competence • **Fear:** Humiliation
3.	**Norming**	3.	**Openness** • Final stage of teambuilding • Amount of honest disclosure • Telling true feelings	• **Feeling:** Likability • **Fear:** Rejection
4.	**Performing**	4.	**High Performance** • Relationships work smoothly in support of tasks	

hrm8c.pmd

1420 Monitor Road • San Diego • California • 92110-1545 • (619) 275-6528 • Fax (619) 275-0324

EFFECTIVE TEAM FUNCTIONING

1. Our Context

Environment
(Outside Impactors)

External/Customers
Internal Constraints
Structural/Rewards
Policies & Procedures

2. What We Do

Values
Mission
and
Goals

Assessment of Current
Status/Future Ideal
Team Mission/Strategies
Vision
Business Plans
Team Goals
Values

The team identifies/clarifies its mission and goals and begins to see their purpose in light of the larger organization.

3. Who Does What

Structure
Roles
Responsibilities

Organizational Structure
Individual Roles and
Objectives
Organizational Structure
Support and Expectations

Team members define the team's interdependencies and determine what tasks require coordination. In addition, roles and responsibilities arre reviewed and expectations clarified.

4. How we Make Decisions
(that Optimize Quality and
Acceptance)

Processes
Systems and
Procedures

Meeting Management
Planning Process
Conflict Management
Rewards System
Problem Solving and
Decision
Making

The team develops procedures for managing meetings, resolving conflicts, solving problems and making decisions.

**5. How Effectively We Work
Together**

Relationships

Work Style
Commuications Style
Strengths and Limitations
Process Skills
Feedback

Working relationships are examined and more productive ways of working together are established.

hrm8c.pmd

1420 Monitor Road • San Diego • California • 92110-1545 • (619) 275-6528 • Fax (619) 275-0324

SMALL UNIT TEAM LEADERSHIP

Team leadership is often determined by team members and can be rotated among members over time.

Team leadership focuses on:

- clarifying the team's overall mission

- ensures the mission is fully understood by members

- provides opportunities for members to determine the best way of fulfilling their mission

- the "why," the "what" and the "when" of the team's work

- letting team members determine the "who" and the "how" aspects of the assignment

Empowered Employees and Empowered Work Teams

The concepts of empowerment advocates a culture in which employees accept responsibility for decision making AND they also accept accountability for the consequences of those decisions and the resulting outcomes.

**Effective Teams
Have Clear
and Agreed:**

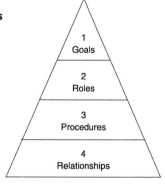

1
Goals

2
Roles

3
Procedures

4
Relationships

hrm8c.pmd

1420 Monitor Road • San Diego • California • 92110-1545 • (619) 275-6528 • Fax (619) 275-0324

MUSTS OF ANYONE'S
MANAGEMENT SYSTEM = TEAMS

It must include:

1. Regular meetings with clear purposes/feedback/actions:

   • with the management team

   • with the organization

2. A "To Do" list of outstanding action items to be followed up on from each meeting, as well as a method to gain feedback on each meeting's effectiveness (i.e., 3 questions: continue; more of; less of).

3. A Performance Management System that fits the manager's style, including clear and agreed upon goals with each direct report (both departmentally and personally).

4. Regular goal setting, coaching, results, and progress review meetings with each individual direct report.

5. A clear and specific coaching and correcting system to deal quickly with performance discrepancies (i.e., progressive discipline).

6. A clear and specific performance review and appraisal system to reward for performance (both results and desired behaviors/culture).

7. An individual - team - and organization wide recognition system to reward positive performance on a timely basis.

8. A specific conflict resolution style (or styles) that are appropriate and effective to both (a) achieve the resolution effectively, (b) maintain/improve the personal relationship.

hrm8c.pmd

continued...

1420 Monitor Road • San Diego • California • 92110-1545 • (619) 275-6528 • Fax (619) 275-0324

MUSTS OF ANYONE'S
MANAGEMENT SYSTEM = TEAMS

9. Inspiring a shared vision/mission and focused set of strategic priorities.

10. Inspiring a shared set of values and a follow-up system to ensure it's being tracked and achieved/rewarded.

11. A well thought out succesion, hiring, and development system to ensure the proper "fit" of people, jobs, and skills.

12. An effective two-way dialog/communications process organization wide to ensure openness in direction setting, surfacing problems and issues, etc.

13. A specific game plan to communicate with and involve key stakeholders and customers on a regular basis.

Question: Which do I do well (circle the #)?

Question: Which 3 - 5 do I most need to improve upon (put a box on the #s)?

Question: What am I going to do differently?

# Above	What	By When?	Comments

hrm8c.pmd

1420 Monitor Road • San Diego • California • 92110-1545 • (619) 275-6528 • Fax (619) 275-0324

EMPOWERMENT CRITERIA

Empowerment Defined
Empowerment is responsible freedom...
A balance of rights and responsibilities.

For a Successful Empowerment Process

1. Need to understand/agree with organization's vision, mission, values, and strategies

2. Need to be proactive within guidelines set - but then given decision-making power, within that

3. Need to still be a team player

4. Need a willingness to be held accountable for your actions/self-initiative

5. Need to be provided with the training and tools to be successful

6. Need management's willingness to:

   - give up some decision-making power/vetos

   - allow some mistakes without punishment

   - provide positive reinforcement/recognition for good empowerment initiatives

   - allow others to come up with "how to" solutions that are different from the ones you would make (as long as the goal is the same).

The Conclusion
Empower individuals (not groups of individuals) when:

- they are personally ready and committed (both person and supervisor)

- the situation dictates empowerment will work

hrm8c.pmd

1420 Monitor Road • San Diego • California • 92110-1545 • (619) 275-6528 • Fax (619) 275-0324

FACILITATING EMPOWERED TEAMS

Unacceptable vs. Participative Leaders

"We seem stuck . . . between two unacceptable alternatives—the leader who dictates to others and the one who truckles to them. If leaders dictate, by what authority do they take away people's right to direct their own lives? If they truckle, who needs or respects such weather vanes?"

—"What Makes a Good Leader?" by Gary Wills
The Atlantic Monthly, April 1994.

What We Need are "Participative Leaders"

"Participative Leaders" are those who gather input
from people on issues that affect them
prior to the decision being made.

1420 Monitor Road • San Diego • California • 92110-1545 • (619) 275-6528 • Fax (619) 275-0324

DECISION MAKING STYLES

"People Support What They Help Create."
—Premise #2

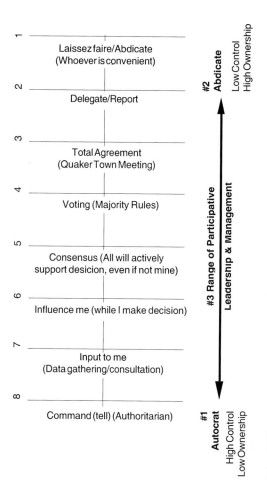

1	Laissez faire/Abdicate (Whoever is convenient)
2	Delegate/Report
3	Total Agreement (Quaker Town Meeting)
4	Voting (Majority Rules)
5	Consensus (All will actively support desicion, even if not mine)
6	Influence me (while I make decision)
7	Input to me (Data gathering/consultation)
8	Command (tell) (Authoritarian)

#2 Abdicate — Low Control, High Ownership

#3 Range of Participative Leadership & Management

#1 Autocrat — High Control, Low Ownership

Consensus Decision Making:
1. is a dynamic and evolving process;
2. means that although it may not the the decision I would make, I'm willing to go beyond living with it to **"actively support"** it;
3. includes an agreement with the decision by the manager/leader who will lead implementation of the decision.

So it follows—Involve people in decisions that affect them ... prior to the decision being made.

Source: Steve Haines

hrm8c.pmd

1420 Monitor Road • San Diego • California • 92110-1545 • (619) 275-6528 • Fax (619) 275-0324

EMPLOYEE NEEDS QUESTIONNAIRE

WHAT DO EMPLOYEES WANT FROM A PERFORMANCE MANAGEMENT SYSTEM?

List in priority rank order (1-10) your needs from your current job.

Priority		Need
Survey Results	Yours	
		1. Higher salary and/or more benefits
		2. Recognition for doing good work
		3. Food, clothing, and shelter
		4. Satisfying the boss' wishes
		5. Promotion to a better job
		6. Personal growth and development
		7. Safety in your work environment
		8. Prestige and status
		9. Job security
		10. Opportunity for independent thought and actions (freedom)

hrm8c.pmd

1420 Monitor Road • San Diego • California • 92110-1545 • (619) 275-6528 • Fax (619) 275-0324

NATIONWIDE SURVEYS (TIME-AFTER-TIME)

TOP THREE JOB "NEEDS" OF EMPLOYEES

1. Recognition for doing good work
2. Freedom for independent thought and action
3. Opportunity for personal growth

OTHER "NEEDS"

4. Higher salary and/or more benefits.
5. Promotion to a better job.
6. Job security.
7. Satisfying the boss's wishes.
8. Prestige and status.

Sources: Dr. H. Migliore, Dean, Oral Roberts Business School, and hundreds of other similar surveys across North America and Europe by Stephen G. Haines.

EFFECTIVE REWARDS ARE ...

- Timely
- Significant
- Personally meaningful
- Competing against oneself only
- Multiple winners

Note: "Pay for Performance" violates all of these. Hence, the need for a different type of "reward"—a "non-financial" reward.

hrm8c.pmd

LEVEL 4 – CREATING A LEARNING ORGANIZATION

Five People Edge Best Practices

16.   Spreading learning quickly.
17.   Institutionalizing Systems Thinking.
18.   Developing HR measures.
19.   Learning from our experiences.
20.   Encouraging creative thinking.

LEARNING ORGANIZATION DEFINED

Gleaning key phrases from a sample of the many definitions in circulation, we see that a learning organization is:

- A system capable of becoming smarter over time.

- A company that continuously improves by anticipating and creating the skills needed for future success, i.e., a business that thrives on change.

- A corporation that maximizes learning opportunities by nurturing and tapping the collective wisdom of its entire workforce.

- A setting where people are constantly, spontaneously learning and applying their knowledge in order to improve the quality of goods, services, work, and life itself.

- An environment where learning is valued as the best, perhaps the only, source of competitive advantage.

- A place, ultimately, where learning has become synonymous with working.

Source: ASTD *Infoline*

> A learning organization is an organization skilled at creating, acquiring, and transferring knowledge, and at modifying its behavior to reflect new knowledge and insights.
>
> — *Harvard Business Review*

hrm8d.pmd

1420 Monitor Road • San Diego • California • 92110-1545 • (619) 275-6528 • Fax (619) 275-0324

ADULT LEARNING THEORY*

"Adults Learn Best by Doing"

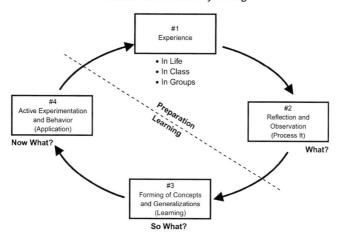

- **Learning is comprised of:** (1) Skills
  - (2) Awareness, knowledge and thoughts
  - (3) Attitude, motivation and feelings

- The application of this learning is your *ability* (or lack-of-ability) to actually put the learning into practice in a more and more *competent way* over time.

- Thus, eventually your abilities to use this learning effectively become *your competencies*.

*Adapted from D. Kolb, "On Management and the Learning Process," in David Kolb, Irwin Rubin, and James McIntyre, *Organizational Psychology: A Book of Readings*, 2nd Edition, Englewood Cliffs, N.J.: Prentice-Hall, 1974.

"Life's Rules of 3"

Application	(1)		(2)		(3)
• Individuals:	Body	—	Mind	—	Spirit
• Learning:	Skills	—	Knowledge	—	Feelings/Attitude
• Human Interactions:	Structure	—	Content	—	Process
• Human Behavior:	Conative (Doing)	—	Cognitive (Thinking)	—	Affective (Feeling)

---

hrm8d.pmd

1420 Monitor Road • San Diego • California • 92110-1545 • (619) 275-6528 • Fax (619) 275-0324

STRATEGIC EDUCATIONAL MODEL (KSA's)

Instructions: Put a High-Medium-Low (H-M-L) in terms of your organization's effectiveness in helping learning occur in each of these 24 boxes.

	Awareness/ Knowledge	Skills	Attitudes/ Immersion	Ability/ Organization Change
VI. Organization-Environment	6	12	18	24
V. Organization	5	11	17	23
IV. Cross-Functional Teams	4	10	16	**Highest Impact** 22
III. Department/ Team	3	9	15	21
II. One-to-One	2	8	14	20
I. Individual	1	**Lowest Impact** 7	13	19

Four Level Model
(for evaluating the effectiveness of training)

—Kirkpatrick

Level 1: Reaction—Did they like it?
Level 2: Learning—Did they learn it?
Level 3: Transfer/Behavior—Did they use it?
Level 4: Results/Impact—Did it make a difference
Note: Consider (ROI (return on investment) as part of Level 4.

hrm8d.pmd

1420 Monitor Road • San Diego • California • 92110-1545 • (619) 275-6528 • Fax (619) 275-0324

HOW TO DEVELOP A HUMAN ORGANIZATION SYSTEMATICALLY

OR . . . LEARNING IS A WAY OF LIFE OR . . . HOW TO SUCCEED AS AN INDIVIDUAL OR ORGANIZATION

Question: What are we doing? What should we be doing?

Levels	Examples	
I. Individual Level	• technical training • managerial training • new hire orientation/ assimilation • job design • O.J.T./cross training	• personal growth • individual career development • continuing education • time management • mgmt. development
II. One-to-One Relationships	• process skills • goal setting performance appraisal • boss-subordinate relations	• coaching/counseling • communication skills • influence, power skills
III. Teams	• staff meetings • team building	• dept. systems & processes • meeting skills
IV. Inter-Department	• design review teams • interdepartmental meetings • liaisons	• integrity mechanisms/task forces • conflict resolution • interdepartmental team building
V. Organization-Wide	• communication systems • HR management system • committees • large systems change	• management conferences • cross-sectional task forces • strategic planning
VI. Organization-Environment Interfaces	• briefings • outside seminars • trade/professional associations	• customer contacts • customer/service training • industry conferences/ publications

hrm8d.pmd

1420 Monitor Road • San Diego • California • 92110-1545 • (619) 275-6528 • Fax (619) 275-0324

DEBRIEFING/FEEDBACK FRAMEWORK

Uses:

1. Projects
2. Incidents/Failures
3. Rollout Changes
4. Etc.

Five Steps		**Goal**
From the Incident ➔	to:	Improvement For the Future*

DEBRIEFING MEETING AGENDA
With Prework: "Completed Staff Work"

Step #1: Goal...   clarity of project objectives

Step #2: What...   happened
in the incident

Step #3: So What...   did we learn
*lots of them

Step #4: Now What...   do we do differently
    *a. to correct the incident
        (recovery strategy)
    *b. to prevent it in the future
        (new systems/processes)

Step #5: Celebrate...   meeting success
* = success above

hrm8d.pmd

1420 Monitor Road • San Diego • California • 92110-1545 • (619) 275-6528 • Fax (619) 275-0324

REINFORCEMENT SYSTEMS

TO SUSTAIN NEW BEHAVIORS

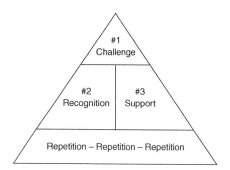

MANAGEMENT AS A PROFESSION

Instructions: Circle what you do now. Then what else you need to do to improve.

____ 1. Resource library, check out

____ 2. Subscriptions:

    ____• newsletters   ____• executive book summary

____ 3. Visual reinforcement symbols (walls, conference rooms, plastic cards)

    ____• slogans   ____• concepts

    ____• models   ____• key points

____ 4. Management networks (just like professional associations)

    ____• buddy systems   ____• management association mtgs.

    ____• bag lunches, films

____ 5. Celebrations of successes, events — re: learnings

____ 6. Skills assessment, development planning (use of assessment tools, surveys)

____ 7. Performance system, accountability

____ 8. Weekly – monthly – quarterly review meetings, mini meetings

hrm8d.pmd

1420 Monitor Road • San Diego • California • 92110-1545 • (619) 275-6528 • Fax (619) 275-0324

LEVEL 5 – FACILITATING CULTURAL CHANGE

Five People Edge Best Practices

21.   Understanding the desired culture.

22.   Developing collective management skills.

23.   Integrating HR with strategic direction.

24.   Designing organizational structures.

25.   Developing change experts/capabilities.

ORGANIZATIONAL CULTURE DEFINED
(The Way We Do Business Around Here)

Organizational culture is a set of interrelated beliefs or norms shared by most of the employees of an organization about how one should behave at work and what activities are more important than others.

Assumptions/Philosophy =
Our World View
("Weltanschauung")
↓
Personal Values
↓
Organizational Values
↓
Norms of Behavior
(i.e., the standards for action)
↓
Individual Behavior
↓ ↓ ↓
**Collectively
Leads to Our
Culture**

hrm8e.pmd

1420 Monitor Road • San Diego • California • 92110-1545 • (619) 275-6528 • Fax (619) 275-0324

ADVERSARIAL CULTURES
WITHIN AN ORGANIZATION

> It now appears that many of
> the problems of communications,
> productivity, and unionization
> lie primarily in the significantly
> different value systems among
> employee populations.

1. Managers versus those being managed

    – or –

2. Line departments versus staff departments

    – or –

3. Manufacturing versus marketing

    – or –

4. Headquarters versus field

    – or –

5. Division versus division

hrm8e.pmd

1420 Monitor Road • San Diego • California • 92110-1545 • (619) 275-6528 • Fax (619) 275-0324

INTEGRATING ORGANIZATIONAL OUTCOMES

DEVELOP AN INSPIRING VISION

"The very essence of leadership is that you have to have a vision.
It has got to be a vision you articulate clearly and forcefully on every occasion.
You cannot blow an uncertain trumpet."

—Father Theodore Hesburgh,
former president, Notre Dame University

The vision lives ... in the intensity of the leader; an intensity that, in itself, draws in others ... and in the moment-to-moment basis of our daily work life.

Three Leadership Tasks

—Adapted from Michael Hammer and James Champy Inc.,

The leader is the inspirer, the motivator, the one who gets people excited about making things happen. Leadership boils down to three simple things:

1.　One is a shared vision

2.　One is communicating that vision; and

3.　One is watertight integrity (if people don't buy into the shared vision, help them find somewhere else to go.)

---

hrm8e.pmd

LADDER OF COMMUNICATION EFFECTIVENESS

(REPETITION – REPETITION – REPETITION)

One-to-One Conversation

Small Group Discussion

Large Group Discussion

Video Conference

Telephone Conversation

Communication Methods	
Words =	7%
Tone =	38%
Body Language =	55%
Total =	100%

What you do speaks louder than what you say!

Conference Call   "2 way"

Voice Mail   "1 way"

Pager

Handwritten Letter

Email/Text Messaging

Fax

Typewritten Letter

Mass-Produced Letter

Newsletter

Brochure

News Item

Advertisement

Handout

We Remember Approximately:

- 10% of what we *read*
- 20% of what we *hear*
- 30% of what we *see*
- 50% of what we *see* and *hear*
- 70% of what we *say* and *do*
- 90% of what we *explain as we do*

Repetition Increases Understanding

- 1st time = 10% retention
- 2nd time = 25% retention
- 3rd time = 40-50% retention
- 4th time = 75% retention

hrm8e.pmd

1420 Monitor Road • San Diego • California • 92110-1545 • (619) 275-6528 • Fax (619) 275-0324

LEVEL 6 – COLLABORATION WITH STAKEHOLDERS

Five People Edge Best Practices

26. Developing global skills.
27. Understanding strategic alliances.
28. Maintaining a positive environment.
29. Creating customer focus.
30. Collaborating with all stakeholders.

Global Leaders for the 21st Century

The development of effective leadership is a major focus of the One Step Beyond/Pacific Center for Leadership programs, which address the characteristics of successful global leaders as defined by the Institute for the Future:

- Patient but persistent
- Humble (as compared to modest)
- Willing to fail and learn from failure
- Possessing a good sense of humor (laughing with, not at, other perspectives)
- Strongly imaginative
- Emotionally stable
- Curious—socially and intellectually
- Perceptually acute, but willing to postpone judgements, sometimes indefinitely
- Capable of listening well
- Intuitive about communication (particularly nonverbal) across cultures
- Comfortable with discomfort
- Comfortable with uncertainty

hrm8f.pmd

1420 Monitor Road • San Diego • California • 92110-1545 • (619) 275-6528 • Fax (619) 275-0324

STAKEHOLDER ANALYSIS

THE WORLD AS A COMPLEX SYSTEM

Stakeholder = any group or individual who can affect or is affected by the achievement of the organization's objectives. The groups listed here are examples of cateogories of stakeholders.

hrm8f.pmd

1420 Monitor Road • San Diego • California • 92110-1545 • (619) 275-6528 • Fax (619) 275-0324

LEVEL SIX -
COLLABORATION WITH KEY STAKEHOLDERS

A "Stakeholder" is any individual or group who "has an interest in, or holds a stake in the work of your organization." By contrast, a 'Customer' is "one who chooses to use your products or services." **A customer is always a stakeholder, but a stakeholder is not always a customer.**

1. Developing the Knowledge and Skills to Operate in a Global Environment
As organizations begin to interact more with representatives of multinational and global organizations, it is necessary to develop and acquire the knowledge and skills needed to be successful in a global marketplace. This includes:

- cross-cultural sensitivity
- foreign language skills
- proper protocol and etiquette
- a clear understanding of the acceptable business practices in other countries
- a sound appreciation for the needs and expectations of foreign customers.

2. Developing and Maintaining Strategic Alliances and Networks
Business is becoming exceedingly complex as customers become more refined and more specific in articulating their needs. Do you have the time and the other resources needed to become skilled in all of the areas impacting your business?

Besides the knowledge you have in your head, there is also the knowledge of knowing where to go to get that which you don't have in your head. That's where strategic alliances and networks are so important—they become a valuable resource pool for the knowledge and skills you don't possess. They also serve as a very valuable reference source for future contacts.

3. Collaborating to Maintain the Positive People Image and Edge
In order for people to perceive your organization as "an employer of choice," they need to be able to see and hear about what you are doing with and for your employees. "Don't hide your light under a basket"—be proud of what you have established in creating a positive people image. You'll attract and retain the skilled workforce needed to build and sustain a competitive business advantage.

There are two very important internal stakeholder groups that you must collaborate with, on a regular basis. These are:

- your employees
- representatives of your employees (unions, associations, etc.)

Seeking and using this input whenever feasible will help to build the positive workplace culture where employee and business issues can be resolved in a harmonious fashion—not through conflict and labor strife.

hrm8f.pmd

1420 Monitor Road • San Diego • California • 92110-1545 • (619) 275-6528 • Fax (619) 275-0324

LEVEL SIX -
COLLABORATION WITH STAKEHOLDERS

4. **Collaborating and Balancing Value Contribution to Employees, Customers, Shareholders and the Community/Society**

The perception of your success as an organization is measured regularly by all of your stakeholders, based on the value that you help to create with and for them.

Employees need to feel that their contribution is valued and that they are being treated in a fair and reasonable manner. Customers need to feel that their patronage and loyalty are valued by you. They also need to feel that they are receiving good value from you in exchange for their patronage. Shareholders expect and are entitled to receive a reasonable return on their investment in your company. Your local community needs your corporate support for many of the special events and projects that are critical in the building of a good quality of life for those who share their lives together— both on and off the job.

Best Practice Organizations work hard to find the proper balance between these varied interests. These are not necessarily mutually exclusive or competing interests. In fact they become collaborative interests when a good balance is established. For many of these stakeholders, the support doesn't always need to be offered or received in financial terms. Contributions of sweat equity, specialized skills and expertise, access to the use of equipment, space or other physical assets all can have a positive value-added impact.

5. **An Intense Customer Focus and Commitment by All Employees**
    *   Each of our jobs is to serve the real customer...or...to serve someone else who does.

    *   There are four levels of a **"Customer Recovery Strategy"** we need whenever a customer is unhappy. Which do we do?

        ___ 1. Deny it's our problem. (I just work here.)

        ___ 2. Fight their concern but eventually give in to them. (They won.)

        ___ 3. Meet their expectations. (Customer is always right.)

        ___ 4. Meet their expectations and then do something else beyond it that they don't expect (including an apology).

hrm8f.pmd

1420 Monitor Road • San Diego • California • 92110-1545 • (619) 275-6528 • Fax (619) 275-0324

"HOW TO" CREATE A POSITIVE WORK ENVIRONMENT

Implementing the "People Strategy" in Your Strategic Plan

Key Points:

1. Best Practices that create this (only if done in an integrated, systems approach)
2. Singular, analytic approaches have been proven not to work.
3. A Positive Work Environment is the same as the culture of an organization - hard to change - highly resistant to singular change attempts such as training alone.

Some integrated approaches that work include:

1. Eliminate fear of failure so the climate or feelings of what it is like to work here are attractive. Innovation is valued and fostered. **Each person has a supervisor who cares about me as a person!**
2. Positive rewards and (self) recognition programs proliferate - including team recognition, thank-you cards and positive celebrations - **effective teamwork is the norm!**
3. Culture change starts with the CEO and top management team and then on to the rest of management - these interactions need to be open, honest, transparent, dignified, respectful, characterized by dialogue, listening, disclosure, integrity, conflict and the search for the right answers from anywhere (NIH is gone).

   If you can't talk about it among management, you can't improve it!
4. Culture change requires support for this positive environment in the media (stories/commu- nications), celebrations for those achieving it, rewards for development by managers, education on how to do it, etc.
5. Employees generally want three things in a positive work environment:

   • opportunity to learn, grow and be challenged,
   • recognition for a job well done,
   • opportunity for independent thought, actions, empowerment, and innovation.
6. Managers are skilled in coaching, mentoring, conflict resolution and participative manage- ment/involvement.
7. The order of the day is "to catch someone doing something right" and tell them.
8. Promotions of management must only consider those who embrace and are skilled in all this.
9. Responsibility is clear and accountability systems (i.e., performance management) are in place and functioning well. People are held accountable (tough love). **However they know what to expect on their job and its priorities.**

   a. And, they are given the training and tools to be a high achiever.
   b. And they are slotted into jobs they have a passion for and the skills to meet the demands of the job/role.
10. An Employee Development Board is in place, functioning effectively and leading a succes- sion planning and career development system for everyone.

hrm8f.pmd

1420 Monitor Road • San Diego • California • 92110-1545 • (619) 275-6528 • Fax (619) 275-0324

SECTION VI
SUMMARY AND HOW TO BEGIN

Option #1
- Make this a major change project. Form an Executive/Employee Development Board—and clarify your vision and values around this.

Option #2
- Conduct a one day Executive Briefing/Plan-to-Plan event—an "educating, organizing, tailoring" and decision making day.

Option #3
- Have us conduct an initial two-day quick needs assessment on People Edge issues and a Executive People Edge Briefing.

Optional #4
- Begin with Succession Planning to identify gaps/needs.

Option #5
- Do a full Strategic People Plan. Use Overview of A-B-C-D to tailor the process to your needs.

Option #6
- Use the assessment of Six Best Practice Levels in this booklet to guide you in beginning to make improvements in 2-4 key competencies.

Option #7
- **Let the Centre be your Leadership Resource Team!**
  Making "Strategic Leadership Development" a major change project and build the "System." Form an Employee Development Board and clarify your vision and values around this.

The employer does not pay your wages.
The customer pays your wages.
The employer merely handles the transaction.
—Henry Ford

A Strategic Formula for Success
1% Inspiration
99% Perspiration
—Thomas A. Edison

---

hrm9.pmd

1420 Monitor Road • San Diego • California • 92110-1545 • (619) 275-6528 • Fax (619) 275-0324

HOW TO GET STARTED IN CREATING THE PEOPLE EDGE SYSTEM? (MANY DIFFERENT OPTIONS)

I. Have the Centre conduct an Executive Briefing (a Plan-to-Plan day)—no obligation, Our *Nothing to Lose Guarantee* is in effect.

_____ 1. Conduct an Executive Briefing and Plan-to-Plan Day with your Executive Team on this topic. It is an "Educating, Organizing and Tailoring" day to ensure our **People Edge System** is tailored to fit your needs and priorities exactly. It comes with our unique '*Nothing to Lose*' guarantee.

II. Begin with Strategic Planning (The Proper and Preferred Way)

_____ 2. Conduct a company-wide Strategic Planning process first, tailored to your specific needs with a People Edge core strategy. Bring it all the way down to Annual Work Plans for each department.

_____ 3. Then form a Leadership/Executive/Development Board (EDB) of senior management to begin to create "The People Edge" core business strategy. Focus its agenda on 2 - 3 people issues first that are most crucial to you.

_____ 4. Have this Board (EDB) develop an organization-wide **"Strategic People Edge Plan"** to support your corporate-wide Strategic Plan's strategy by building and installing our People Edge System.

III. Begin Succession Planning (You win the game on hiring and succession, not on development alone)

_____ 5. Start doing succession planning by beginning with the executive team positions at first, and later moving the process down to other key levels/positions.

_____ 6. Install a career development, coaching and mentoring program to support these succession and development processes. Begin with the executives taking a coaching course together as a team.

_____ 7. Reevaluate and modify your recruitment, hiring and orientation/assimilation processes (i.e. Smart Start) to ensure you hire the right people as well as ensure they start off with the right values and desired culture of your organization.

IV. Begin Performance Improvement (Day-to-day accountability and consequences)

_____ 8. Redo your Performance Appraisal form and procedures to provide accountability and to reward contribution to achieving your core strategies and adherence to your core values.

_____ 9. Help revamp your entire Performance Improvement/Management System; starting with your executive and management levels. This will ensure a tie-in to your Strategic Plan and taking it down to the individual accountability level as noted above.

_____ 10. Audit and recommend modification to your entire formal and informal pay and rewards/ recognition system to ensure they reinforce and support your future directions.

hrm9.pmd

HOW TO GET STARTED IN CREATING THE PEOPLE EDGE SYSTEM?

V. Use Our Six Levels of Leadership Competencies (360° Needs Assessment/Evaluation)

_____ 11. Clarify your Vision of what type of leadership skills, styles, and behaviors you want in your organization, and tie it to the specific roles of executives and managers. Use our Six Levels of Leadership Competencies as a starting framework.

_____ 12. Conduct an initial organization-wide **Leadership and Business Acumen Needs Assessment** in order to define your needs better. Use our two 36 and 30 question surveys respectively to conduct the assessment and to prioritize your first steps in leadership development.

_____ 13. Conduct a 360° degree leadership evaluation of yourself or your executives using our Six Levels of Leadership Competencies (and 30 skills) in order to model desired leadership behaviors. Use the results to develop Individual Development Plans (IDP's) for each person.

_____ 14. Use our **Centering Your Leadership**SM _"Board Game that teaches"_ and its 408 Leadership Best Practices questions and answers to form the core of your kick off a systematic **52 week Leadership Development Program**.

VI. Conduct Some Training (Lowest value beginning)

_____15 Conduct a **"Train-the-Manager/Trainer"** course and program so that some managers can become better trainers as well. Use this cadre of trained managers to help conducting **"People Edge"** courses throughout the organization later on.

_____ 16. Conduct cross-functional teamwork training and team building for new or ongoing teams in the organization today. Start with specific problem projects.

_____ 17. Conduct specific leadership or People Edge management workshops on topics urgent to your business (such as conflict management, coaching, teamwork, cultural change, Systems Thinking, etc). Use our list of **Six Natural Leadership Competencies and 30 associated Leadership Skills** to identify the course(s) needed.

—and also—

VII. Let the Centre Be Your Leadership and People Edge System Resource Team (mastery expertise = better value)

_____ 18. Making creating a **"People Edge System"** a major change project and let the Centre assist you in building the "System". We are experts in all of these options on how to begin.

Hiring the Centre as your part-time project oriented master consultants and trainers is more cost effective than full-time staff (no benefits, salaries or office overhead costs).

hrm9.pmd

Page 149

PROPOSAL - PEOPLE EDGE
We Want to Be Your Leadership/Management *Resource Team*

Benefits to Your Organization
1. **A People Edge Strategic Plan and Leadership Development System will be in place** to ensure a comprehensive assessment and matching of desired organizational competencies and employee needs…a win-win situation.
2. Management and supervisors will **have the developmental opportunities** needed to ensure they become first class managers and leaders…and you will have the talent ready to assist your growth and future needs when you require them (not afterwards).
3. The **lack of need for a full-time senior executive in charge** of this, along with no office space or employee salary and benefits, means that this is a more cost-effective approach.
4. By centralizing current spending in this area, you may find that **extra cost is not even necessary**.
5. The **adult learning cycle** is utilized to maximize the transfer of real learning (i.e. *adults learn best by doing*).
6. The *in-house* **Train-the-Trainer and team approach** helps to build teamwork, positive values and cultural norms, more open communications and a "management language.'.
7. The end result is a more highly skilled, cohesive management team that can **achieve your Vision and your Strategic People Edge objectives** …now and into the future.

Research-Based Best Practices
1. The American Quality Foundation in Texas, and Ernst and Young in Canada recently completed the most exhaustive research on organizational success. **Increasing your range, breadth, and depth of leadership skills and practices** was one of only three Best Practices that always resulted in greater organizational profitability, success, and market share.
2. Our extensive People Edge Best Practice areas show none of our eight key authors and well known HR experts had our Six Best Practices HR areas and only two had even the beginnings of a Systems Approach.
3. The Centre's proposal is based on extensive research of over 25 prominent authors and 30+ books on the topic of leadership development. These Best Practices were translated, interpreted, and integrated into our own comprehensive Systems Thinking Approach to Leadership Development presented in this proposal.

Features of the Centre's Leadership Development System
Strategy #1:   Establish a Management Structure
1. **You establish an Executive Development Board** composed of senior management with Human Resources and Training support in order to guide and control all decision making and direction for the *Resource Team*.
2. **A Centre Master Consultant and Trainer will be the Coordinator/Facilitator** in charge of our *Resource Team* and also be responsible for the Centre's delivery and achievement of the Executive Development Board's desired goals. The Executive Development Board will be completely in-charge as the leaders of this effort.
3. **In-house administrative support** will be needed to coordinate the day-to-day activities and logistics.

Strategy #2:   Develop a Strategic People Edge Plan
1. Your **Executive Development Board** (EDB) will sponsor a Strategic People Edge Plan for the organization with our support and expert advice.
2. A **Succession and Development Program** will be set up in a cascade fashion, top management first.
3. **In-house administrative support** will be needed to coordinate the day-to-day activities and logistics.

hrm9.pmd

continued

1420 Monitor Road • San Diego • California • 92110-1545 • (619) 275-6528 • Fax (619) 275-0324

PROPOSAL - PEOPLE EDGE
We Want to Be Your Leadership/Management *Resource Team*

Strategy #3:   **Assessments of your Development Needs**

1.   We have and use a number of **different online** Leadership/Management and Executive Development (i.e. Business Acumen) **assessment tools** that can be adjusted as necessary.

2.   We can also conduct **360° assessments** tailored to your needs and desires **online** as well.

Strategy #4:   **A Tailored Leadership Development System - Daily and Weekly**

1.   We will jointly tailor this **Leadership Development System** to your specific needs including key Human Resources involvement. Our Centre's Leadership Development System is quite flexible and might include:

   •   **Specific Individual Development Plans** for each participant as the cornerstone of the system

   •   **360° Feedback Instruments online**

   •   **Seminars and Workshops** on needed topics once the assessments are completed—both in-house and external university-type options

   •   **Train-the-Trainer workshops** to train *your* personnel to deliver the needed courses (with less and less of the Centre's support over time).

   •   In-house trainers could include staff and line executives to maximize learnings in the organization.

   •   **Comprehensive support materials** and lesson plans to easily transfer these courses to your personnel.

   •   **Different needs and seminars** for different levels of executives, management, supervisors.

   •   Other **development options and practical work projects** will be emphasized as well as in-house seminars and skill building practices.

   •   Ongoing reviews by your Executive Development Board will be conducted to ensure the developmental progression and the fit and integration with your succession planning needs.

Strategy #5:   **Strategic Thinking and People Planning**

1.   This *resource team*'s activities will be tightly **tied to your Strategic Plan** and your Strategic People Plan.

2.   **A long term plan for this System will be developed** in order to ensure that "bite-sized," year after year developmental attitude becomes part of the fabric of the way you do business.

Strategy #6:   **Extensive Centre Resources**

1.   **Books, materials, assessment instruments and lesson plans will be made available** through the Centre's extensive copyrighted material (over **5000** pages in eight volumes of our own copyrighted Best Practices), as well as other recommended publishers depending on the topic.

2.   **The Centre's 12 Master Consultants**, Facilitators, and Trainers collectively offer courses in all 30 different skill areas of Leadership Development. No other firm can offer both this comprehensiveness **and** our Systems Thinking Approach.

3.   The full range of **Centre resources** are available for courses in order to be completely flexible with your delivery needs, styles, and dates .

4.   See our **full People Edge Product Line** (Models on our new Systems Thinking Press website (www.systemsthinkingpress.com), Assessments, Executive Summary Articles, Executive Briefing Booklets, Workshop Participant Notebooks, and eight volumes of Tool Kits and Reference Guides) for more detailed information.

hrm9.pmd

EMPLOYEES LEARN WHAT THEY LIVE

If an employee lives with fear, he learns to avoid risk taking.

If an employee lives with deceit, she learns to stretch the truth.

If an employee lives with small expectations, he learns to have a limited scope.

If an employee lives with a heavy hand, she learns to beat the system.

If an employee lives with ridicule, he learns to keep his ideas to himself.

If an employee lives with formality, she learns how to be a bureaucrat.

If an employee lives with mistrust, he learns to be suspicious.

If an employee lives with hostility, she learns how to fight.

If an employee lives with indifference, he learns not to care.

If an employee lives with appreciation, she learns to make an extra effort.

If an employee lives with leadership, he learns how to take initiative.

If an employee lives with openness, she learns how to be honest.

If an employee lives with experimentation, he learns how to be innovative.

If an employee lives with clear values, she learns how to set priorities.

If an employee lives with customer respect, he learns how to provide outstanding service.

If an employee lives with encouragement, she learns to be confident.

If an employee lives with positive visions, he learns how to perform miracles.

If an employee lives with challenge, she learns how to master change.

Jim Clemmer, in *"The V. I. P. Strategy"* 1988.
Inspired by Dorothy Law Nolte's poem *"Children Learn What They Live"*.

hrm9.pmd

1420 Monitor Road • San Diego • California • 92110-1545 • (619) 275-6528 • Fax (619) 275-0324

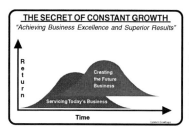

THE SECRET OF CONSTANT GROWTH
"Achieving Business Excellence and Superior Results"

ENHANCE YOUR "STRATEGIC IQ"™!

The Centre's Executive Briefing and Plan-To-Plan is designed to establish a common set of principles and knowledge on the specific Strategic Management project that your organization needs to develop or improve. By using this Systems Thinking Approach™ and principles, you can develop an Enterprise-Wide Game Plan for successful execution. Build your capacity to achieve and sustain business excellence and superior results.

Achieve Organizational Clarity, Simplicity and Superior Results!

EXECUTIVE BRIEFING DAY OUTLINE

AM - Executive Briefing : *"Educating and Assessing"*
- Choose from eight Strategic Managment Topics
- Learn the research on Proven Best Practices
- Assess your organization vs. these Best Practices Management Topics

PM - Plan-To-Plan Tasks: *"Organizing and Tailoring"*
- Organize and engineer success up front
- Tailor the change process to your needs
- Build a practical and realistic "Game Plan"

EIGHT EXECUTIVE BRIEFING DAY TOPICS
Strategic Management: The Systems Thinking Approach™

1. Strategic and Systems Thinking

2. Reinventing Strategic Planning

3. Enterprise-Wide Change

4. Creating the People Edge (Strategic HR Management)

5. Achieving Leadership Excellence

6. Becoming Customer Focused

7. Aligning Delivery & Distribution (Business Planning)

8. Creating Customer Value (Positioning & Design)

Science-Based Proven Research
- We are Interpreters and Translators of Proven Best Practices Research from the *Science of Living Systems*.
- We tailor these Best Practices into powerful, practical and easy to use, simple tools.

THE SYTEMS THINKING APPROACH™
- We own Systems Thinking Press™ the "Premier Publisher and Clearinghouse for Systems Thinking Resources".
- Visit our web site www.SystemsThinkingPress.com
- Learn about ALL our Strategic Management Materials.

NO FURTHER OBLIGATIONS
- There are NO Further Obligations after this day.
- WE will work with you ONLY if we are convinced you are seriously committed to success (why waste time & money)
- Success requires your understanding, discipline, persistence and leadership!

Systems Thinking Press™

Specialists in Systems Resources
www.SystemsThinkingPress.com

Send Order Form to: Systems Thinking Press - 1420 Monitor Road - San Diego, CA 92110-1545
Phone: 619-275-6528 - **Fax:** 619-275-0324 - **Email:** info@SystemsThinkingPress.com - **Website:** www.SystemsThinkingPress.com

Date _____ If rush order, need products by _____

Name _____ Title _____

Company _____

Shipping Address _____

City _____ State _____ Postal Code _____ Country _____

Phone _____ Fax _____ Email _____

Quantity	Code	Description	Regular Price	Amount
	EBHRM	Creating the People Edge through Strategic Human Resource Development	call for rates	
			Sub Total	
			Sales Tax (CA residents only)	
			Shipping/handling charges	
			TOTAL (payable in US $)	

Payment Method ~ Please Check One

Credit Cards (processed in US Dollars)   Visa   MasterCard   American Express   Discover

Credit Card # _____ Expiration Date _____

Name on Card _____ Signature _____

_____ Check or Money Order Enclosed   _____ Purchase Order (only for over $100)   PO# _____

Shipping: Please choose a shipping method below. We make every attempt to ship the cheapest and best method. If you wish to be contacted with the shipping cost prior to your order being shipped, please check here _____

United States
- UPS Ground – 1 ½ weeks/less
- UPS Three Day (business days)
- UPS Two Day (business days)
- UPS Next Day (business days)
- US Postal Service

International
- Federal Express
- UPS
- US Mail

- International – One week or less
- International – One week or less
- Global Priority* - 1 ½ weeks or less

- Priority International* – 2-3 days
- International Expedited* - 2-3 days
- Global Express* - One week or less

* Not available in all areas.

Return Policy

You may return the products within 30 days of receipt for a refund (eProducts are not refundable). Shipping charges will not be refunded. A 20% (or greater) fee may be applied for items returned damaged. To assure proper credit, you must do three things: 1) return materials by a traceable means, 2) include a copy of your invoice, and 3) provide a reason for the return.

Our "Nothing-To-Lose Guarantee"

Our unconditional guarantee of high quality materials: if for any reason you are not satisfied with any of Haines Centre Assessments' materials, you may return them within 30 days for a refund – no questions asked.

We reserve the right to change prices without prior notice.

Systems Thinking Press
1420 Monitor Road · San Diego · CA · 92110-1545 · (619) 275-6528 · Fax (619) 275-0324
www.SystemsThinkingPress.com · Email info@SystemsThinkingPress.com